On the Role of the Actuary
in a Changing World

John R Gordon Bsc FIA

Published by Dolman Scott Ltd

ISBN: 978-0-9564307-0-0

For my Father, whose wisdom has never sought Professional qualification but has always been a source of inspiration

CONTENTS

1.   Background and Scope

This paper is my first foray into actuarial authorship, and I anticipate it will be my last.

Choosing to write a paper such as this about the role of my Profession is not a decision I have taken lightly, and it is no coincidence that I chose to do so in the midst of the biggest economic crisis the World has faced in my lifetime. For while there are few views expressed in this paper that I would not have proffered before the crisis broke, the scale of events we have witnessed has undoubtedly lent greater urgency, if not greater credibility, to some of its principal arguments.

The paper's objective is to critique the purpose and direction of the Profession in the context of a world whose priorities are changing. As such the paper has two interwoven narratives.

The first is a critique of the wider socio-economic situation and the role of the Financial Services industry in the aftermath of the financial crisis and in the context of challenges that lie ahead and the changes that are likely to ensue.

The second is a critique of the Profession's present vision, strategy and efficacy in the context of those changes, and an examination of what the Profession could be doing to improve its profile, better support its public interest obligations, expand its influence and, more pertinently, better orient itself to navigate the stormy seas that lie ahead.

As a critique, if the paper is to be of value it must inevitably contain some degree of criticism: if I thought the Profession did have a clear sense of purpose and direction, did understand the implications of the changes we are now beginning to witness and was striking an appropriate balance between the commercial interests of its members and the long term public interest, I would not be writing this.

Instead, I look around and I see too much complacency, both inside and outside the Profession, at the scale of the challenges we face. I see beliefs that too many otherwise intelligent people have allowed themselves to accept as truths, and I see many issues that should be being given greater priority.

This paper is essentially a wide-ranging assault on the thinking and practice that has brought us to the present point. As such it may seem less like a ramble through the actuarial countryside and more like a trip to the actuarial dentists, as I seek to poke, prod and scrape into the deep, dark corners that lie behind the Profession's public smile.

I am under no illusion as to how this may be viewed by some of my Professional colleagues. The result will, I expect, leave me accused of many things - arrogance, temerity, precociousness, presumptuousness, insolence or disloyalty all seem possible - but at least a lack of ambition should not be among them.

Ambition, however, comes in many forms. I haven't written this paper to advance my career (it won't), I haven't written it for personal pleasure (it wasn't), and I haven't written it because my employer thought it a good idea (as no employer would, and I am self-employed).

That I have written it at all is largely as a matter of Professional and humanitarian conscience. As the dentist always tells us, check-ups are worthwhile even when they don't lead to any remedial work, and after much merger chewing it could be argued that the Profession is now ripe for one. In which respect while my credentials as a dentist have yet to be tested, the check-up is at least free and the advice can readily be ignored.

As such, I hope that the paper will be received in the spirit in which it is offered. By that I mean a) that I hope the Profession will be prepared to credit the paper's subject matter with enough legitimacy to find it worthy of discussion, and b) that if, as I expect, the conclusions from that discussion broadly follow the 80/20 rule, that the Profession will not let a desire to discredit the bulk of the paper's proposals detract from a focus on what it proposes to do about the remaining 20% to which it might struggle not to attribute some merit[*].

Few will agree with all that I write, just as few will disagree with all that I write. Between those poles views expressed span the spectrum, from those that are contentious to those that might readily find consensus. In all cases, where I express an opinion it is because I believe it to be in the public interest or the Profession's interests for me to do so.

As a point of principle, in any instance where the Profession's interests and the public interest could be construed to be in conflict I give precedence to the latter. For while I agree with the sentiment, drummed into me on the day I first enrolled, that every man is a debtor to his Profession, it is equally true that every Profession is also a debtor to society – and in that respect, I regret to say, my Profession's debt is presently running at levels that I find morally compromising.

In consequence, I do not doubt that some will regard this paper to be detrimental to the Profession's interests. My alternative position is that the Profession has a history of avoiding discussing subjects that it fears may prove detrimental to its interests, that this fear is paralysing its discourse, and that this is in itself acting to the detriment of both the Profession's interests and the long term public interest.

My premise is that it is better to confront contentious subjects than to avoid discussing them. In doing so I am less passionate about my conclusions being endorsed than I am about the Profession conquering its reticence and actually engaging on the issues.

---

[*] It is not that I think only 20% of my ideas will find any currency. I simply note that, as the merger process has shown, the Profession's present mode of governance supports inertia even when a majority are in favour of change. In which respect I am crudely estimating that around 20% of what I propose might have resonance among enough members for there to at least be a constructive debate about it.

In the aftermath of the protracted merger debate and a failed merger vote, I struggle to maintain my optimism that the Profession has the capacity to adapt. In some respects the challenges the Profession faces have never looked greater. If there is another organisation that has talked more about change and delivered less, it is not one with which I am familiar. Yet, on the principle that it is better to have tried and failed than not to have tried at all, here I am writing a paper that has the need for change as its central theme.

Radical change, too. In the last section in particular I explore a number of more esoteric areas in which our actuarial skills and way of thinking could be deployed to greater public benefit. While accepting that many will find such proposals a stretch too far, by including them I invite reflection on their relative worth in comparison with some of the activities that presently occupy much of our time. I also invite consideration of the extent to which the pursuit of short term objectives may be compromising the Profession's long term vision, and of the extent to which the pursuit of commercial interests may be limiting the Profession's collective investment in matters of long term public interest.

I strongly endorse the view that the World needs actuaries, or to be more precise the view that the World needs people who have the kind of skills that actuaries' typically possess. But whether those skills are presently being utilised to best effect is another matter. I believe that as a Profession we need to invest our skills, training and intellectual capital rather more wisely than we presently do if we are ever to convince a sceptical public that it needs us – and objective which, to judge by the rhetoric of successive leaders over the years, the Profession attaches some importance to.

As papers on matters actuarial go, there are few conventions that this one does not break. Technical content is minimal, which will doubtless be a disappointment to some. In similar vein philosophy, psychology and general reasoning may seem like poor substitutes for rigorous actuarial analysis to some. To which my only riposte would be that rigorous actuarial analysis didn't stop us getting into the present mess, and it will not get us out of it.

One benefit of this approach will I hope be to make the paper accessible to non-actuaries as well as to actuaries. Indeed, given that a substantial part of the paper's subject matter is of relevance to a wider audience this was one of my main aims in writing it. A popular criticism of our Profession over the years has been that its members often speak in terms that others do not understand. If this paper is perceived as a small step towards redressing that balance then all to the good.

The paper poses more questions than it answers, for the simple reason that I don't have all the answers. Where I feel in a position to make recommendations I do so, but I don't regard the lack of an answer to be a good enough reason for not asking a question. The paper is intended to provoke thought and discussion. It is not a mandate for either a new Actuarial Profession or a New World Order, though I admit to passionate advocacy of both.

Other departures from tradition are in the paper's scope, and in its style. Scope is wide, commensurate with the paper's ambition, and its style is commensurate with what I perceive to be the gravity of our present situation: it is not evident to me that the Profession's penchant for tact and diplomacy has served it well in recent years, and I adopt neither here.

That the paper has certain recurring themes, and makes certain recurring points, is intentional. Some points bear repeating. Please accept my apologies in advance for any offence to Professional sensibilities that doing so may cause. Those of traditional outlook or sensitive disposition should perhaps look away now. Alternatively, you might wish to spare yourself a good deal of plain English and simply refer to the paper's précis.

I make no great claim of originality or insight in respect of the paper's content or the credentials of its author. I do, however, have faith in the relevance of its subject matter. It is my belief that the Profession has allowed itself to be distracted from what is important at a time when it can least afford the luxury. Change is upon us, whether we like it or not. Will the Profession look to the future and help lead that change, or will cling to the past and instead find itself dragged along in change's wake?

If it is to be the former, open minds, new ideas and a fresh strategy are the least that is needed. If it is to be the latter, the Profession had better prepare itself for a rough ride down the road to obsolescence.

For those who persevere, it is my hope that this paper will give cause for reflection, perhaps from a different perspective to that normally afforded by the day job, on what we do as individuals, what we do as a Profession, and why. It is my hope that from such reflection the change in attitude and direction that I believe our Profession so badly needs might yet still emerge.

2.   The Wider Context

It may not be good politic to note it, but we live in a dysfunctional society.

If this was a sociology paper – interestingly enough, a box into which one of the initial Institute reviewers categorised it – I would explore the subject in rather more detail. However, as it isn't, and at the risk of doing a disservice to years of more learned research, I instead offer this brief synopsis of the malaise that I believe sits at the heart of our modern society: *too many of its members, beyond the bare essentials of their existence, have a connection with the World that is exercised largely through their bank account and a flat screen monitor.*

It is a measure of our society's dysfunction that so many of its members view the World primarily as a marketplace in which to acquire things. So ingrained has this notion become that possessions, and the means to acquire them, seem to have become our principal – and for many people only - benchmark of social status.

Moreover the dynamic by which society empowers the agents that govern it ensures that the scale of dysfunction isn't just perpetuated, but accentuated. A socio-economic model whose definition of success knows only one measure will of course tend to promote those it believes are best placed to deliver against that benchmark. It is no coincidence that those who captain our industries and form our Government often tend to be even more driven to accumulate wealth than many of those they lead.

The social trends that have brought us to the present point (globalisation, the pre-eminence of greed, the fragmentation of communities, increased focus on self, the rising cult of celebrity and the growth of cyber-society) are all well-documented elsewhere so I won't dwell on them here. What is of relevance going forwards is what consequence might flow from the increasing stress to which the society they've delivered is going to be subjected.

One consequence of these trends is that many people have become increasingly disaffected by, and disengaged from, what one might colloquially call 'real world' problems. Even among those who are still engaged, there is a tendency to regard the big challenges we all face as someone else's responsibility to resolve. Such complacency is further fuelled by the faith that many still hold in the power of innovation and technology to address those problems without the need for any personal sacrifice or infringement of their own lifestyle choices, a belief that is as misplaced as it is convenient.

Adding to the dysfunctional fray is the central role that our present financial system plays in influencing socio-economic policy. Despite mounting evidence of the folly in so doing, our present generation of policymakers continues to dance to the tune of volatile financial markets, still apparently unaware that to serve the long term public interest - as is supposed to be their obligation - they need first to quit the dance floor and invest in some better music.

Thus has modern society created its own virtual reality, a reality that has thus far allowed the issues and risks considered later in this paper to be largely downplayed, and an illusion that has thus far managed to keep our society firmly on the path towards its own destruction.

It is to the discredit of our present generation of political leaders that they have failed to acknowledge or engage with people on the true reality of our present situation.

It is also to the discredit of the Actuarial Profession that it continues to acquiesce when confronted by such short-term thinking. The Profession, it seems, out of either a misguided sense of its own interest, deference to commercial interests or a conveniently blinkered view of what constitutes the public interest, feels compelled to dance to the same discordant tune. Whatever the reason, this is an abdication of leadership that I believe undermines the Profession's risk management aspirations and amounts to a betrayal of the Profession's own public interest mandate.

Financial markets should be a servant of the people, not their master, but any objective review of the experience of recent years would struggle to conclude as much. This matters, because if our society and its economy are to stand any chance of surviving the scale of change that is to be visited upon them, reform of financial markets is essential.

Our industry appears to have become a caricature of our economic system's worst excesses (more on which later). Those who think its ills can be cured by better governance alone should take a closer look at the profile of the financial transactions that characterise today's financial markets, scratch beneath the glossy surface of incremental tax revenues and take a look at what *real* value those transactions are adding. If they do, they will find little that is contributing to the greater good and much that is serving to undermine it.

Few voices inside the industry have thus far been bold enough to call the bluff of those who tell us that a booming City is vital to the well-being of our economy, and few voices have thus far been bold enough to say that it needs to be cut down to size. It is telling, though, that the present FSA Chairman's voice is among them. When even the FSA is proffering the view that some parts of the City have grown too big for society's good, financial sector profits are too high and that a number of its activities are socially useless, one begins to believe that change may be afoot.

Such views are easier to express, perhaps, when you are a gamekeeper not a poacher - as Lord Turner would know, having successfully played both – and while he only speaks the truth, at a time when so many others still seem to be choking on it he is to be commended for doing so. It is a small step in the right direction. No surprise that all the usual suspects have lined up to offer their criticism, but the point has been made, and many outside the industry would agree with him.

<u>The Need For Change</u>

I will make a prediction. Not a particularly bold one, in the circumstances, but nevertheless one I hold with some conviction: without a fundamental change in economic thinking, fundamental reform of financial markets and a fundamental reappraisal of social priorities, and at the hands of one or more of the influences I touch upon in section 5, at some point over the next few decades our present socio-economic system is going to collapse.

When it does, while both past precedent and human nature suggest that hopes of an orderly transition to a new socio-economic system may be optimistic, that is not to say that our degree of preparedness does not matter. Prospects for a less destructive transition could at least be enhanced if, instead of refusing to countenance that the present model is unsustainable right up until the event that proves it, Government and policymakers would engage with people of vision, on a global scale, to map out the alternatives.

The difficulty is that human nature has bestowed upon most of us an instinctive resistance to countenancing that we may have got things wrong, or to accepting unpalatable truths that run contrary to our own beliefs. Gaps in the evidence are sought and exaggerated, alternative explanations are offered. Thus, for example, can otherwise bright people see cold snaps as evidence against climate change, otherwise bright clergymen choose creationism over evolution, otherwise bright CEOs blame the failures of their companies on anyone other than themselves, and otherwise bright politicians continue to insist that we are winning wars that many others without a vested interest can see that we are losing.

Only when all other avenues have been exhausted is truth finally confronted, and even then some politicians, business executives and religious leaders seem capable of maintaining an impressively resilient state of denial.

Nowhere is this more manifest than in the attitudes of some of those who lead our own industry. Ex-CEO Dick Fuld may have collected $40 million a year for the privilege of being at the Lehmans helm, but he still couldn't bring himself to accept any responsibility for the ship having sunk. His defence? He considered he'd acted properly on the basis of *what he had been told.*

The insight offered by Fuld's observation is particularly pertinent, because some people in the higher echelons of Business and Government are not inclined to listen much even when they *are* told. Indeed it seems some people who lead our industry can react quite badly to being told, because they have grown rather used to doing the telling. The result, among other things, is that many of our companies have become rather dysfunctional places to work, a subject I explore in more detail in section 8.

Those who subscribe to the Fuld school of management are products of a flawed system, having evolved vestigial ears that are receptive only to certain types of message. They think not of long term sustainability but of short term profit. They talk outwardly of employees, but think inwardly of headcount. They don't build teams, they build empires, and they reign over them like emperors. They are very accomplished at justifying their rewards, reinforcing their self-image and promoting their own interests. And as Fuld himself has shown, they are very adept at finding others to blame when things go wrong.

In a wider sense, their cause is aided by another very human trait: *the greater our collective investment in a particular perceived truth, the more reluctant we tend to be to relinquish it*. In which respect, there has scarcely been a greater human investment in anything than the investment made by successive Western governments in the doctrine of Capitalism and in the centrality to our society of the principles of wealth creation and economic growth.

This helps to explain why some of those who drive our industry have been allowed to perpetuate their ideology for so long. Despite the growing list of industry failures piling up in their wake (some are considered elsewhere in this paper, but for a good flavour see the list of public interest provocations included as an Appendix to this paper), we continue to place faith in their ability to govern, continue to subscribe to their tired arguments about the need for big financial incentives and continue to allow ourselves to be convinced that we are at risk from a flight of their talent.

Thanks in no small part to the present financial crisis, however, the general public now have a rather better grasp of reality than most of those who lead Government, industry and perhaps even our own Profession give them credit for. Yet like addicts who have knowledge of their problem but see no solution, what they lack is a coherent vision of a better future. In its place grow recrimination and cynicism. If the root causes are not addressed both will continue to grow, to destructive effect.

In the meantime, we find ourselves in a curious situation where many realise that our present socio-economic system is flawed to the point of being unsustainable, yet nobody in any position of authority dare say as much for fear of the consequence.

While the Profession has been contemplating its merger navel, our wider society has continued inching closer to its tipping point. Assuming that democracy itself is not a casualty of the coming collapse, our present socio-economic model will only be sustainable for as long at least half of the voting populace believe that the continuing quest for prosperity upon which it is built *is in their own interests as individuals*. In which respect it is becoming increasingly difficult for people to maintain that belief. As worldly constraints begin to bite further in the years ahead, this trend looks likely to continue.

In this context, perhaps the proponents of Capitalism's greatest success has been to convince so many for so long that it is a system that will indeed bring benefit to all. Yet the financial crisis and its aftermath has created many more losers than winners, and there is no disguising the fact that the model itself is on collision course with the rather more tangible but less tractable realities of global population growth and increasingly scarce resources.

Cosmetically at least, little thus far appears to have changed by way of adaptation to the consequences of this new reality. Talk of green shoots is back, share prices are up, the property market seems to be bottoming out and banks are making large profits again. Traditionalists could be forgiven for thinking that they have weathered the worst. Yet the underlying realities *are* changing. There is a growing understanding that technology and innovation cannot provide all the answers, that growth cannot continue untrammelled, that politicians are being economical with the truth, and that we are about to enter an age of enforced austerity. And when the full implications of that come home to roost, a large amount of resentment is going to be looking for an outlet.

This will have a fundamental impact on Government, on industry and on society as a whole. Modern society, aided by the economic doctrine that supports it, has created a culture that has traditionally seen affluence as a measure of success. The switch to a culture where affluence is seen instead as a symbol of *excess* will be subtle in its means but profound in its effect.

It is subtle in that it has already started, but is being misread by many as just the usual disaffection that comes with downturns in the economic cycle. It will be profound in that, while today it is mainly bankers and politicians who are loathed, in the age of austerity that awaits us those who flaunt profligacy, in all its guises, are likely to join them.

The fabric of society is being stretched as never before. While politicians may never have been held in particularly high esteem, they have surely never been less respected than they are presently. What should worry us is that while 'detached from reality', 'lacking in vision', 'resistant to change' and 'serving their own interests, not the public interest' are routine labels for today's generation of political leaders, they apply just as readily to many of our industry leaders, and for that matter on present form could in some respects just as easily be used to describe our own Profession.

This should be more than just a matter of mild concern. Revolutions have been built on less.

Ultimately, from the wreckage of our failing system a new, rather less destructive socio-economic vision will emerge, though quite what pain society will go through before it does remains to be seen. In the interests of minimising that pain we should be planning for the transition now. It is a transition that will require unprecedented levels of global co-operation if it is to be successfully managed.

The principal agent of change will be the encroachment of a new reality, one that no amount of Government obfuscation or industry denial will alter. Alistair Darling, Win Bischoff and friends may still talk of growth, but the planet is kicking back and the growth game is almost up, a subject I explore in more detail in section 6. Any further growth Britain achieves will largely be at the expense of less developed nations, in the guise of either supporting them or exploiting them, depending on your point of view (the title of Bischoff's recent report [1] on the future of our industry, sponsored by the

Treasury - "UK *International* Financial Services – The Future" – in effect concedes as much).

At the level of nation states such tribal tendencies, and the pursuit of self-interest that characterises them, sit at the heart of much that is wrong with the World. The simple truth is that when the chips are down people – and the Governments that represent them – tend to think local, not global. Recent evidence of that extends well beyond Bischoff's report. The Government's recent use of anti-terror legislation to freeze Icelandic assets and the 'British jobs for British workers' mantra that recently resurfaced again are good examples, while the Profession's merger preoccupations show that it isn't only Governments that can become myopic in times of crisis.

In today's increasingly globalised World with its increasingly globalised problems, tribal thinking is not progressive thinking. It has much destructive potential, because it greatly enhances the risk of wider catastrophe at the hands of one or more of the threats noted in section 5. Global co-operation is the *only* answer, yet it is becoming increasingly clear that we cannot rely solely on either Governments or industry to provide global leadership.

The Future of UK Financial Services

What does all this mean for the future of our industry?

Your view of that will probably depend on your view of many other things. If you subscribe to the Win Bischoff view of reality, there is little wrong with our industry that being more competitive cannot cure.

In many respects, Bischoff's report – endorsed by the Treasury - is a shocking document. Not least, it is shocking in its degree of detachment from so many other people's reality, shocking in its confirmation that industry bubbles can be just as delusional as property bubbles (and far more resilient), and shocking for the fact that it mentions competition over 50 times, growth 36 times, but fairness only once and the need for more global co-operation hardly at all.

Before the financial crisis broke – in no small part because people like Mr Bischoff have been telling them for years - many people believed that we already had a competitive UK Financial Services industry.

And in a way, indeed we did. Competitive salaries; competitive bonuses; a competitive tax system; a competitive regulatory environment. The market also had more players than it has today, which as the free marketeers will tell us is in itself good for competition.

In short, competition was apparently rife. Yet still our financial system came close to collapse. Is this not telling us, in the clearest possible terms, that competition is not the issue?

What people like Mr Bischoff do not appear to recognise is that competition comes in many forms, not all of them good. The real reason for the expansion in UK Financial services in recent decades, as has now been laid bare to a far bigger audience, has nothing to do, as Bischoff's report suggests, with the UK's reputation for 'competence, responsibility and trustworthiness', and everything to do with having made the UK environment 'competitive' - for which read making the UK a home for easy credit, big bonuses and low tax rates. In an age of free-flowing capital, labour and information, and at a time when we talk global in so many other ways it is really an affront to people's intelligence for representatives of our industry to claim otherwise.

Here, in simple terms, is an example of how Bischoff-style competition works in today's Financial Services industry:

1) In each of the World's financial centres, promote the notion that to attract the best people you need to pay them large salaries and incentivise them with large bonuses
2) Hope that at least one of them subscribes to that view
3) When they do, use the fact to convince the others that they risk a flight of talent if they do not follow suit

Quite what degree of fairness this brand of competition might deliver ought to be apparent even without the knowledge that some of its greatest proponents have just brought our industry - and with it the World economy - to its knees.

Most observers who don't have a vested interest has long since recognised that some sectors of the Financial Services industry have been transgressing the boundaries of fairness in their over-zealous pursuit of short term profit for years. Yet the Bischoff report offers no proposals for market reform, no initiatives to clip the wings of volatile financial markets and has little to say about the causes of the present crisis.

For Mr Bischoff and his fellow disciples know only one language. Given the contribution it makes to sustainable global development and the greater good, it might as well be Welsh. In fact, outside the bubble of their (and our) own industry it would probably be better for their (and our) reputation if it *was* Welsh.

It may be a bitter pill for many of us who have spent a good chunk of our working lives supporting it to swallow, but Financial Services will continue to be a pariah industry for as long as those who lead it continue to defend the indefensible. Which in turn will be for as long as people like Mr Bischoff are allowed to run it.

The industry needs a new generation of leaders who talk a language that the rest of the people in a changing world can empathise with. A generation that sees no problem with the principle of wealth creation, but understands that we need a rather more balanced definition of wealth. A definition of wealth that encompasses more than just the acquisition of material things for the simple reason that the World is running out of materials for us to acquire, and a definition of wealth that somehow places value on waking up each morning to survey something other than an environmental wasteland.

This generation will understand that what we need is far more global co-operation, not more global competition. This generation will see the moral vacuum behind big bonuses, because this generation will understand that the big problems of the developed world are not so much being addressed by a corpulent Financial Services industry as being compounded by it. This generation will understand that if people outside the Financial Services industry can do a good job without being paid a big bonus, so can those inside it.

At the heart of the debate about the future of Financial Services sits a basic question: do we want an industry, and thereby and economy, whose fortunes continue to be tied to the whims of people who are forever peddling their assets around the globe in search of the lowest tax rate and the softest opportunity to make a short term profit, or do we want to rebuild it around longer term objectives more closely aligned to pursuit of the common good?

The Bischoff report provides an unambiguous answer to that question - but unfortunately not a progressive one.

In the long run our industry, like our Profession and our society, faces a choice: adapt or die. In which respect the sooner it can rid itself of dogmatic dinosaurs like Mr Bischoff and his ilk, the better.

The Profession's Role

What questions does this raise about the Profession's role?

Well, as considering that question forms a large part of the subject matter of this paper I will not explore that in any great detail now. I will, though, make some general observations.

Over the years I have come to appreciate that my own brand of plain English is not particularly well suited to the Profession I chose to join. Having read the opening few pages of this paper you may well have reached the same conclusion rather more quickly. However, notwithstanding my limitations as an exponent, and recognising that diplomacy undoubtedly has its place, when I look at the challenges that now confront us and I reflect on the place to which the Profession's own brand of discourse has brought us, I remain convinced that a fundamental change in approach is needed. Diplomacy of course has its place, but only in benign times is diplomacy on its own an effective agent of progress, and for the Actuarial Profession benign times are now consigned to its past.

To illustrate the point, here are some observations that you will not hear made by the Profession: the Bischoff report is misguided; a significant fraction of the City's activity is socially useless; Capitalism is failing us; the increasing degree of polarisation in the distribution of wealth is undermining the stability of our society; without a change in direction our society is heading for a big fall; the reputation of the Financial Services industry is being destroyed by its bonus culture; our present economic model is unsustainable; our financial markets are no longer fit for purpose; as a Profession we should have spotted and highlighted the financial risks that precipitated the banking crisis.

I could go on, but you get the gist. There are a number of such provocations in these pages, which may help to explain the reception this paper received at the Institute (hence its external publication). For ours, it seems, is a Profession whose moral backbone is never more exercised than when being contorted to keep its head below the parapet of contentious debate.

The Profession might also struggle to admit that it was not just banks and the global economy that had a bad year in 2008. That it was also a bad year for the Actuarial Profession may not have registered in the consciousness of many, but that is only because the Profession itself does not register in the consciousness of many.

Aside from the merger debacle, our Profession's collective intellect, vision, long term outlook, expertise in risk assessment and detailed knowledge of the financial services sector did not manage to translate into any effective warning about the risks that precipitated the present crisis or their potential impact. Meanwhile press coverage of events surrounding James Crosby's departure from the FSA not only dispelled the notion that actuaries don't get involved in running banks, but inferred that when they do so they can do it just as badly as anyone else. And the aftermath of the crash has highlighted just how little the Profession has to say about matters of profound public interest.

All of which hints at one fundamental role our Profession could be fulfilling, but isn't. If we are to have an opportunity to address the kind of structural and human frailties that have delivered this and previous financial crises before they deliver the next one, we must first acknowledge those frailties, and secondly we must discuss and agree how best to manage them. Bear that in mind as you read this paper, and clock the number of concerns I touch upon that are scarcely acknowledged by the Profession as issues, let alone discussed in any meaningful way.

I of course recognise that the Profession as a whole is not in a position to engage in the kind of discourse I adopt in this paper. But neither is it tenable for the present degree of near-paralysis to continue without adverse consequence either. It ought to be clear by now that this is not an effective way for the Profession to either expand its influence or fulfil the kind of ambition that routinely graces the speeches of those who lead it.

I also recognise that it is not in the Profession's gift to single-handedly address the many issues touched upon in this paper. But is it not incumbent upon a Profession with global representation and a duty to serve the long term public interest to promote global co-operation and support the move to a more sustainable mode of existence in any way that it can?

"These are times when the World needs actuaries, even if the World does not yet know it". So said Ronnie Bowie from the midst of the crisis, in his Presidential address to the Faculty on 6th October 2008[2], before adding that if we are to answer that need we "would have to show a boldness and a spirit of enterprise for which we are not currently renowned".

I agree, on both counts. But what the World does not need is actuaries doing more of what we've been doing in the recent past. Today's World is a world in crisis, and it needs actuaries to be deploying their skills in rather more effective ways.

What is going to change to make the World think it needs us?

Anyone who has listened to the speeches of successive Presidents of Institute and Faculty over the years would not accuse the Profession of a lack of self-esteem, but of more importance is the esteem in which it is held by those it purports to serve. If the Profession is not already counselling opinion about that, perhaps it should be. The results might provide it with a much-needed wake-up call.

In the absence of a change in approach, the Profession seems destined to continue to be caught out by risks that it either mismanaged, did not recognise or simply chose not to highlight. In the wake of future events, it is going to become increasingly untenable for a Profession that purports to have such vision, such risk management expertise and such passion for defending the public interest to retain its credibility.

For these reasons I believe the Profession will need to be far bolder and far more receptive to change than has been its tradition if it is to prosper in future. In particular the Profession must bring greater breadth, depth and clarity to its discourse, and if it wishes to convince a sceptical public of its worth it will need to back up its fine words with rather more convincing deeds. And if it thinks it will be able to achieve this simply by providing its individual members with training and development opportunities it is fooling itself, as any objective review of its recent history should be enough to confirm.

In truth, however, there is much more at stake than this. The present course our society is charting is untenable, our present position is unstable and the only long term outcome that can be predicted with any confidence is that wide-ranging economic and societal changes are going to result. The Profession could benefit by recognising as much and finding a voice with which it can help to lead the change agenda.

If that change doesn't come soon enough, and if the Profession continues to maintain its present introspective focus, it may yet find itself - along with so much else - buried in the rubble.

3.   The Merger Process: A Case Study

I had intended to make only passing reference to the proposed merger between Institute and Faculty in this paper, but that was because I'd assumed that ultimately common sense would prevail and the UK Profession's membership would, when at last given an opportunity to vote on the matter, choose the common sense option.

That vote was held as the first draft of this paper was nearing completion, and regrettably common sense did not prevail. A 71.6% vote in favour in any normal referendum would be decisive, indeed any politician could only dream of such a level of support, but for the Institute of Actuaries with its dated voting rules it was still not enough.

The merger process and its result may have achieved little else, but it has provided a convincing demonstration, if it were needed, of just how ill-equipped the Profession's current decision-making process is to cope with the challenges of a fast-changing World.

In an age when the World is struggling to come to terms with the effects of Globalisation and a large scale financial crisis, it is depressingly symbolic that our Profession has spent so much of the last two years trying to bridge 400 actuarial miles between London and Edinburgh. That might have been more forgivable had anything eventually changed as a result. It is rather less so given that it didn't.

I have much sympathy for those who have worked tirelessly to drag our Profession to clear post-merger water only to find their efforts compromised by those who would sooner see it silenced through thirst than see it drink, but the views of the minority must be respected. It is not their fault that the Institute's voting rules gave their view more credence than it warranted, any more than it is their fault that only 60% bothered to vote (another indictment of the process and the Profession, and a matter for serious reflection given how many man-hours were collectively invested in getting us to that point).

As for the unsolicited intervention of a minority who attempted to prejudice the vote, I presume they are grateful that not all of us with strong opinions took it upon ourselves to foist them upon others by sending unsolicited emails en masse. Otherwise their views might just have been drowned out in the cacophony (and as an aside, I found it a fitting irony to a shambolic process that the merger's most vocal critic was himself a Fellow of both Institute and Faculty).

Was the outcome a surprise? Sadly not. When it comes to recognising the need for change or the need to act, in any group of people there will always be a minority who will refuse to accept it. There was no reason to suppose that as actuaries we should be any different, and the merger process has proved as much. For that reason the Institute's present rules and protocols are a recipe for paralysis. And to the outside world – or at least to that portion of it that is still minded on occasion to look in our direction – paralysis is largely what they witness.

If you believe, as I do, that the Profession's desire to accommodate all interests is reducing the effectiveness with which it serves the most important one, perhaps the most prescient observation one could make about the merger experience is that if the UK Profession has a need for division it is on grounds of ideology, not on grounds of history or geography. A division between those of us, both north and south of the artificial divide, who wish to be members of a progressive, forward-thinking Profession and those that are happy with the one we've got; between those who recognise the gravity of our current situation, recognise the importance of a public profile and wish to be members of a Profession that actively contributes to public discourse, and those who don't; between those who are preoccupied with form and those who are more interested in substance; and between those who are happy with the Profession's present course and those who see it as slow suicide.

If that cannot be achieved within the rules of the existing Professional bodies, it is perhaps time that the progressive majority in both Faculty and Institute collectively resigned their membership and joined a new club whose mandate and voting rules better reflect the demands of the times.

It would then be for the remainder in both Faculty and Institute to decide where their best interests lie. Those who are happy to drown with their traditions can hardly complain if the majority choose a different ship by way of alternative. It would certainly be a strange kind of democracy that required the rest of us to join them. Freed from our burden, those who remain can then be left to consult with each other on as many subjects as they choose for as many years as may suit them.

As the residual minority left in old Institute and Faculty would no doubt still resist merging with each other, and in an effort to spare them the months of discussion that would undoubtedly ensue about what they might call their new joint-venture ship, I offer this suggestion by way of alternative: *Two Institutions Traditionally Averse to New Initiatives & Change.* As well as aptly summarising the sense of history and strength of tradition that this fraction of the Profession's membership retains, it also provides any third party minded to engage in discourse with them an idea of what to expect, and has the added advantage of collapsing down into a fitting 7 letter acronym that gives a suitable indication of the kind of future that would await them.

For the rest of us, that would surely be a better prospect than the one we are presently greeted with. On the back of its failed merger attempt, today's Profession looks more out of touch than ever, trapped in a degenerative cycle of introspective discussion, division and reflection that seems destined to deliver ever-dwindling influence and keep it firmly on the road to obsolescence.

The World is changing, and a majority in our Profession recognise the need for us to change with it. The merger process and its outcome therefore leave the UK Profession to reflect on how it is ever going to be able to move forward, or indeed agree a line on anything, if the wishes of the majority are perpetually to be held hostage to the views of a minority.

Having a UK Profession that speaks with one voice - or for that matter with any voice - might only be one small step down the road to bridging the gap between the Profession's aspirations and its present reality, but it is a necessary one.

If the Profession really is incapable of reinventing itself and finding a voice, in the interests of managing expectations it would be better for it simply to recognise that fact and curtail its rhetoric. The grand visions of tomorrow will remain just that if they continue to be met with impotence today, and what use is the Profession's talk of boldness and enterprise if it is never to be translated into its actions.

As for the merger process itself, the sooner the Profession can learn from the experience and move on, the better. In the history of Professional endeavour, has there ever been another time when so many large brains have been constrained by so much small-minded thinking for so long? I doubt it.

If the World had been witness to events within the UK Profession this last two years, it may well have concluded that it does indeed need actuaries – but only for their entertainment value, and only for that portion of its people who are too old to watch a proper pantomime or too busy to watch a proper soap opera.

From here, in a UK actuarial context at least, one must hope that things can only get better.

4.   A Historical Perspective

A Brief History of Me

Among other things, writing this paper has given me cause to reflect on the history of my own involvement with the Profession. And while the last thing I want to do here is to bore you with stuff about me, a little of that history might prove helpful in giving some personal context to the perspective I present in this paper.

I joined the Profession back in 1985. That seems a while ago now and time is a great distorter, but I do recall that my rationale for joining wasn't particularly deep or particularly well-reasoned. A flatmate had applied to work for a consultancy firm in London. It was a job that sounded like it would suit a maths grad, the pay was OK and the long term employment prospects looked good.

A quarter of a century later, the rest is history. Small decisions beget big consequences, and my ex-flatmate has much to answer for (the man himself, incidentally, had within a year seen a strange kind of light and left to train as an accountant).

While my staying power proved greater than his, in the end I too left the company, in 1991, for three main reasons: 1) I'd had my fill of working in London, 2) I'd just qualified and was ready for a change, and 3) it had become clear to me by then that my own interests and those of my employer were not particularly well aligned. In one of those curious twists of fate, I hadn't even begun looking when I got the proverbial phone call.

Thus began 9 years on the payroll of the life & health industry, after which experience I left to join a charity. That probably sounds far more altruistic than it was - the charity position was still a financial services role, it paid pretty well and it was just across the road from where I'd previously been working.

Five years later, in 2005, by which time I'd realised that it wasn't just spending too long on the payroll of insurers that left me susceptible to creeping institutionalisation, I decided to become self-employed. Perhaps the most liberating aspect of that experience was being released from the influence of everyone else's visions and values for long enough to better understand my own.

For better or worse, you are now reading the result.

A Brief History of the Profession

The history of the UK Profession is well-documented elsewhere and I don't intend to dwell on it unduly here. Nevertheless, to give some context to this paper's subject matter I think it is helpful to keep a summary view of that history in mind.

As was the case in many other fields, Britain once led the world both in the development of insurance and in the development of Actuarial Science. Reflecting on that today, in an age when knowledge and information have gone global, that might seem rather academic. But our traditions are interwoven into that history, and our Profession's present standing and direction - and to a degree perhaps even our own perceptions as individual actuaries - have been shaped by it.

What follows is not intended to be an exhaustive list, but set out below are some of the key events in that history:

    1762   Equitable Life founded, the term 'actuary' first used
    1848   Institute of Actuaries founded
    1856   Faculty of Actuaries founded
    1920s First mortgage endowment policy introduced
    1962   First unit-linked policies introduced
    1977   First low cost endowment mortgage policy introduced
    1978   Actuaries role expands into general insurance
    1982   Appointed Actuary role introduced
    1988   Personal Pensions plans launched
    1991   First Structured Investment products appear on the UK market
    1994   Pension mis-selling review begins
    1999   Mortgage Endowment mis-selling review begins
    2000   Equitable Life forced to close to new business
    2003   Appointed actuary role abolished
    2005   Morris Review of Actuarial Profession published

Using a selection of such snapshots to surmise our history is in a way as unsatisfactory as using the fossil record to represent the variety of life on Earth, but it at least gives a flavour of some of the main events. No bias is intended, and in the case of our own history many of you will be at least as well-qualified as I am to fill in the gaps – feel free to do so as you see fit.

When I look at this list, two things stand out.

The first is the accelerating pace of change in recent decades. The last thirty years or so in particular have seen a vast expansion in both the level and diversity of Financial Services activity. This expansion has now been with us for so long that we have come to regard it as normal, and synonymous with progress.

The second is the fallout that appears to have accompanied this trend. The pace of change and rapid expansion has, it seems, extracted a price.

But my list, as you may have noted, is not quite up to date. And the most recent event to warrant inclusion might yet prove to be the one that shapes its future course more than any other. It warrants a closer look.

5. Actuaries and the Modern Economy

The Crash of 2008

'Banking Crisis' and 'Credit Crunch' were the most popular labels initially used to describe the greatest financial crisis the World has faced in many years. It remains to be seen what label history ultimately settles upon, but I do hope it finds something more fitting.

Others have already given a far more detailed explanation of the specific triggers for the crisis than I could provide in these pages. Those who are particularly interested might wish to refer to Francis Pereira's recent article in The Actuary [3] or to a transcript of *The Economist's Inaugural City Lecture,* delivered by Adair Turner back in January 2009.

That the last twelve months have clearly been disastrous for the World economy and for the banking industry is self-evident. But to cast the present financial crisis purely in banking terms would be misleading. For a more honest appraisal of what isn't working one must look beyond symptoms, and beyond their immediate causes, into the deeper malaise that sits at the heart of our present financial system.

While the Government's response to the crisis has undoubtedly been radical in terms of the scale of intervention and its cost to the taxpayer, it has not thus far been particularly radical in any other respect. With an election looming, plenty of money has been found - or printed - to stoke the stalled twin engines of consumption and growth, with the aim of getting the economy back on the rails again as quickly as possible and restoring Britain Plc's journey to ever-increasing prosperity.

This is short-term, simplistic, complacent thinking. I doubt there is much more sympathy for Fred Goodwin and his ilk within our ranks than there is outside them, and deservedly so, but he was surely right when he observed that reckless bankers are not solely to blame for the mess we now find ourselves in. For in truth the underlying forces that delivered failing banks to us are not only alive and well, but rather more widespread than most outside the banking industry might like to believe.

Headlines cast in black and white play to a populace that has little time for shades of grey. In this age of convenience people prefer their truths to be simple, and our democratic process has long been following tabloid headlines down the path to meeting that need, to the point where the democratic process itself now seems to be dictated more by soundbite than by reasoned debate. In that respect it is no surprise that bankers should now find themselves demonised, but to do so risks masking the underlying problems.

To view the World in this way is to miss the subtle textures that define most of its problems. Soundbites are the enemy of reason. Not all MPs are on the take; not all bankers are bad; not all actuaries are good; not all civil servants are inefficient or incompetent; some actuaries do work for banks, and for all their Professional training and experience can still occasionally make disastrous decisions of headline-making proportions when doing so; the same people can sometimes make disastrous decisions when they don't work for banks, too. Across the Atlantic, America's most reviled institution is not a bank but an insurer, one that recently posted the biggest loss in US corporate history, and one whose troubles were rooted more in London than in New York.

While soundbite solutions may treat symptoms and may get politicians elected, they are no cure for our socio-economic ills. In that respect, the remedies that have thus far been used to treat the financial wounds inflicted by the present crisis differ from those used in previous crises only in their scale. Throwing money at banks and the economy treats only symptoms, and better governance or stronger bank regulation will treat only symptoms; as I seek to explore in more detail later, the underlying problems run much deeper.

In fact, not only has reform to date been minimal, and not only do all the structural weaknesses that precipitated the present crisis still remain, but ironically the sheer scale of the financial fallout from the current crash may well have served to undermine the task of addressing them. When the symptoms are so severe that they risk killing the patient it is understandable that they should attract most of the attention. The danger is that by the time the patient is faring better people will once again have lost interest in treating the disease, a risk compounded by our Government's own seemingly addictive dependency on one of the more beneficial short-term side effects of the condition. Yet if the disease isn't treated the patient's next relapse could well prove fatal.

In a wider context, the spectacle of so many of the parties who did play a role in fomenting the present crisis being so quick to point the finger but so reluctant to look in the mirror has been as unedifying as it was predictable. With Government blaming bankers, bankers blaming regulators, regulators blaming rating agencies, rating agencies blaming Government and any number of overspent, over-borrowed consumers blaming everyone but themselves, the only thing all those culpable seem to agree on is that none of them saw it coming. Which highlights the other attraction of symptoms over causes: they are much easier to treat, because they are much easier to see.

There is, however, one respect in which the outcome of this crisis has already differed from those that have preceded it. The nature and scale of this particular crisis, and the media coverage that has accompanied it, has succeeded in turning any number of laypeople into armchair financial experts. Soundbite solutions may not have gone completely global, but we can be sure that they permeate many an irate British household, and they are being fuelled by people's (not unreasonable) belief that many of those who contributed most to the problem are not reaping their share of the consequence - a sentiment reinforced in the public psyche, fairly or otherwise, by having to witness some of the biggest culprits walking away with knighthoods and big pensions rather than criminal records.

All of which has served to create much surface noise to detract from informed debate of the principal problem, which is that the crash wasn't just symptomatic of bad bankers or bad governance, but of systemic failure on a grand scale.

What is the actuarial view on all this? Well, from the little that the Profession has thus far said on the subject it seems that it too, like Government, considers that there is little wrong with our present financial system that better governance cannot cure.

As for what form that tighter governance should take, the Profession appears to regard that as a discussion for others to have. Instead of seizing a golden opportunity to contribute to a wider policy debate on the need for financial reform, the Profession seems instead to have conveniently characterised the crisis as largely a banking problem, thereby justifying its relative lack of discourse on grounds that 'actuaries don't do banking'.

And it is not just in its discourse that the Profession's response has been characteristically disappointing in its lack of ambition. A working party (the Global Financial Crisis Group) was set up with the limited mandate of exploring the causes of the crisis and 'providing information to members' on its implications for the management of risk. To gauge from its output to date and the banality of its updates, progress made by the Group thus far has been equally limited.

From a Profession with over 20,000 members that prides itself on its long term vision, moral backbone and understanding of finance and risk, it has been a truly feeble response. Even if the present crisis could be convincingly cast in purely banking terms, would it not be appropriate for the Profession to engage in public discourse given the scale of the impact it has had on so much else?

In a wider context, the argument in support of a passive stance on all matters of policy that are deemed to fall outside the Profession's immediate areas of responsibility might be defensible on grounds of theoretical principle (though that would require a very narrow interpretation of our public interest responsibilities, as I explore further in section 7), but it cannot be so easily defended on the basis of what it has brought us: a collapsing economy, an industry in disrepute, a Profession whose reputation and influence is dwindling and a public who increasingly see us - when they see us at all - as symptoms of the condition not as agents for a cure. Strong reputations are not built on such weak foundations. If as a Profession we are as enlightened as we claim to be, we have an odd way of showing it.

It seems to me that there ought to be some point beyond which matters of public interest become important enough to render any debate about the appropriateness of passing comment upon them rather semantic. It also seems to me that we have already reached that point.

If the most far-sighted passenger on board the Titanic had seen that the ship was heading straight for a large iceberg, one would hope they might have mentioned the fact despite their lack of navigational responsibility. Certainly with the benefit of hindsight there would have been plenty with cause to wish that they had. As we are the Profession with the long term financial vision, our fellow passengers on the ship UK Plc might be forgiven for wondering why we too fail to spot large financial icebergs.

More specifically, events leading up to the 2008 Crash confront our Profession with an unpalatable choice of truths. Either we are collectively not as smart at managing financial risk as we would like others to believe, or the mechanisms we have in place as a Profession for ensuring that such risks are highlighted and brought to the attention of policymakers are not working. Which is it?

Personally, I find the notion that no actuaries were aware of the reckless lending that some banks were indulging in, no actuaries understood the inherent risk profile of the particular type of structured investment vehicles that repackaged that debt, and no actuaries were in a position to question the assumptions of the agencies that rated them to be lacking in credibility.

Assuming that some in our number did understand the risks, perhaps we should be asking ourselves what exactly it is about our Profession's culture, structure and policy that prevented that knowledge from translating into any tangible benefit. It ought not to be good enough for us to simply hide behind the notion that 'actuaries don't do banking', when it is quite clear that some of us do, and when it is quite clear that some of the underlying issues permeate well beyond the banking industry.

For obvious reasons, the Profession is keen to promote its credentials in the growing field of risk management. But if this pitch is to have credibility rather than be seen as an exercise in convenient opportunism, are not the financial risks that precipitated the present crisis just the kind of risks we should be demonstrating our ability to recognise?

We are far from alone in choosing silence as our preferred form of diplomacy on some matters of public interest, of course, but any comfort we might seek in numbers surely ought to be tempered by the degree to which our Profession trades on its virtue as a defender of that interest.

In similar vein, while humility too seems to be in short supply elsewhere that ought not to excuse our own Profession's lack of it. At a time when the Profession's words and deeds have never seemed more mismatched, am I alone in growing tired of listening to moral backbone-slapping rhetoric extolling our own virtues and reminding ourselves why the World really does need us?

While visiting the LSE shortly after the crisis broke back in November 2008, the Queen asked one of her hosts, Professor Luis Garciano a simple but challenging question: why didn't any of the so-called financial experts see it coming? Eight months later the Queen duly received a formal response from a group of eminent economists. The letter concluded: "In summary, your Majesty, the failure to foresee the timing, extent and severity of the crisis and to head it off, while it had many causes, was principally a failure of the collective imagination of many bright people..."

It would be difficult to disagree with that observation. Perhaps more insightful, however, was Professor Garciano's personal reflection when being asked about the letter, which we can safely presume was equally well-considered: "I think the main answer is that people were doing what they were paid to do, and behaved according to their incentives, but in many cases they were being paid to do the wrong things from society's perspective".

Quite so. But that is a response that hints at a rather bigger problem. The Queen might have asked an obvious follow-up question: what, therefore, is changing to ensure that people are incentivised to do the right things in future?

Suffice it to say, on evidence to date, that the answer would be both brief and require rather less reflection on Professor Garciano's part. If anything, the situation in the banking sector has got worse, not better, with minimal reform to date and a reduction in competition leading to fatter margins and bigger profits for the players that are left.

Professor Garciano's observation is hardly a new insight but it is a hugely pertinent one. The malaise to which he alludes is widespread. Indeed it manifests in the incentive schemes of no small number of actuaries.

That would appear to leave the Profession somewhat conflicted. Incentives linked to short term profit are not in the long term public interest, yet a significant fraction of the Profession's membership still subscribes to them, and the Profession's current strategic priority is to support the interests of its members. This is one subject, perhaps, upon which our silence as a Profession has reason beyond mere diplomacy.

If the Profession wishes to improve its image and reputation there are some simple steps it could take, a subject to which I return in section 10. But first that will involve confronting some unpalatable truths. Not least, for example, accepting that not only did some of our number understand the risks, but that as a Profession we have been happy to condone, and as individuals in many cases happy to actively exploit, the kind of practices to which Professor Garciano refers and which are seen as having been instrumental in helping to foment the present crisis.

Little is ever learned from a state of denial. The same resistance to admission of individual culpability, in a wider context, is translating into a powerful collective resistance to change, resistance which a weak Government with distorted priorities and much historical baggage of its own is demonstrating little appetite to address.

My own view is that the issue highlighted Professor Garciano is just one of a number of weaknesses in our economic and financial systems that helped precipitate the present crisis, including the following:

(i)   An economic system that prioritises the creation of wealth above all other considerations
(ii)   A financial system whose focus is short term profit growth
(iii)   An industry-wide incentive and reward system that reinforces delivery of (ii)

(iv)   A market dynamic that is increasingly being driven more by sentiment than economic fundamentals

(v)   A proliferation in the range and complexity of financial products without corresponding understanding of the underlying risks and interdependencies

(vi)   A growth in appetite for speculative investment and an expansion in the range of investment instruments that support it

(viii) A corporate attitude to risk management that focuses more on specific risks than generic risk, emphasising the attention given to risks that might affect a company's *relative* industry standing, and limiting the attention given to risks that also affect the competition or the economy as a whole

Government acquiescence has clearly also played its part. In the boom before the bust the Financial Services industry was the jewel in the Government's financial crown. In the wake of its stellar growth issues of regulation were played down, governance issues were ignored, greed was indulged as an as an agent of enterprise and profligacy tolerated as a by-product of success. All of this helped to create a climate where any dissenting voices could easily be ignored. As indeed they were.

The past tense may be premature, but how quickly sentiment has changed. It is now clear to many outside the industry, if not inside it, that the limitations of our financial system extend well beyond a few badly-run banks. Furthermore the scale of the accompanying bust is going to ensure that it lives in the collective memory for a long time, and the protracted payback is going to ensure that those culpable will not quickly be forgiven or forgotten.

One of J K Galbraith's lesser-quoted observations in the aftermath of the 1929 crash was this: "Who is to make wise those who are required to have wisdom"[4].

If we have faith in our own virtues, one of our greatest attributes as a Profession is our collective wisdom. The present crisis has shown, in spectacular fashion, the scale of its absence on occasion both in Government and around the Boardroom tables of any number of large financial institutions.

Looking back on the events of 2008 it is still difficult to comprehend quite how close the global banking system came to collapse, and it still surprises me how little thus far seems to have changed as a result. Many have lost their jobs, the property market has taken a fall, our currency has taken a hammering, the nation has had to spend mind-bogglingly large amounts of public money and the public has lost a large amount of confidence in both Government and the Financial Services industry's competence to look after their interests, but none of that seems yet to have translated into any material long term consequence for the industry that blew in the storm, or for many of those who were meant to be supervising it.

Early days, perhaps, but we still have unrestrained financial markets, we still have highly-leveraged capital markets, we still have banks who play both the casino and the high street, we still have a short term bonus culture, we still have Boardrooms setting remuneration policy, we still have the conditions for housing boom and bust, and we still have largely the same regulation. Depressingly, on a larger scale we also still have weak Government and a Financial Services industry that is light on humility and heavy on hubris, and on a smaller scale we still have a Profession that has no voice and a preoccupation with its own internal affairs.

Among its other consequences, however, what the Crash of 2008 has provided is a very real context for people to ask relevant and searching questions about the nature of our current financial system and the economic model that supports it. Those questions are being asked, but they have not yet been met with convincing answers. What is still missing is a respected independent voice with a sufficiently clear vision and a sufficiently long term view to inform and articulate a considered policy response.

If only it could find the boldness and clarity of purpose to do so, there is surely a role for the Profession to play in this respect, one that would allow it to both raise its profile in a positive way and make a worthwhile contribution to a subject of profound public interest.

Regrettably, boldness and clarity of purpose are qualities not readily associated with today's Profession. There are plenty of good reasons for it to discover them quickly.

Lessons from the Crisis

One of the more noteworthy early consequences of the 2008 crash was the seismic impact that the ensuing loss of confidence had on financial markets. Gripped by uncertainty, volatility increased dramatically as rational analysis succumbed to the vagaries of human temperament. In a triumph of sentiment over substance, greed, fear and the herd instinct prevailed, their signature flowing boldly and freely in daily currency, commodity and share price fluctuations around the globe.

If the Crash of 2008 could be regarded as an outlier, a one off incident whose reverberations will eventually be subsumed by a return to economic normality, this might not unduly concern us.

However it is my contention that this is not the case.

Clearly the specific combination of circumstances that precipitated this particular crisis *are* unique, but if one looks to the future there is little to reassure that there will not be a repeat, on similar scale or worse. Far from being a one-off threat to our economic stability, it seems likely that the present crisis as merely a portent of greater challenges that lie ahead.

The truth is that our underlying economic and financial model is fundamentally flawed, and the present crisis and its aftermath are merely the latest – and thus far greatest – manifestation of the frailty of its condition.

That condition is terminal. Our financial system is going to be tested by a combination of hard-hitting events the like of which it is has not yet previously experienced and the scale of which it is not equipped to withstand.

Consider the following risk factors and their potential impact:

1) continuing global population growth
2) global warming
3) peak oil followed by global fuel shortages and an energy crisis
4) shortages of food and water
5) escalation of conflict
6) widespread civil unrest, leading to disintegration of social structures
7) global pandemic
8) major terrorist event (biological, chemical or nuclear attack)

In the above list, population growth is evidently less a risk than a reality. I include it because of the central role it plays as an exacerbant of the rest. Global warming and resource shortages are what one might call primary risks, in that their likelihood and potential impact are both high and largely independent of the other entries on the list. The risks of global conflict, widespread civil unrest and the disintegration of social structures are themselves dependent to a considerable degree upon the extent to which the primary risks are successfully addressed, while the risks of global pandemic and terrorism are largely but not exclusively independent of the rest.

Threats such as these present too depressing a prospect for most people to think about, and their very intractability offers a good excuse for anyone seeking a reason not to. Including actuaries.

For while one could argue that the Profession is as well-equipped as anyone else to quantify the potential impact of such risks, in practice the presumption seems to be that as these are the kind of risks that Government is elected to manage on our behalf. In other words the Profession can confidently, if conveniently, set the boundaries of its public interest responsibilities to exclude them, and thereby avoid having to invest time in considering them.

The flaw in this logic is that the big problems ultimately impact all of us, and by ignoring them we are entrusting others to properly assess and effectively manage them on our behalf. Adopting such an approach is a considerable act of faith, one that a review of recent evidence would do little to substantiate.

Beyond the potential scale of their impact, however, the other challenge such threats present is the limited extent to which they are capable of being reliably factored into our risk assessment models. Only the last two entries typically feature in our capital adequacy assessments, and there is considerable uncertainty attached to any assumptions made even for them.

Have another look at the list. Think about the likelihood and potential impact of each risk and ask yourself how compatible it is with the one in 200 year risk framework we use to test capital adequacy. Also ask yourself how well-equipped you believe our present economic model is to withstand the financial storm that would ensue, even if we were afforded the luxury of each risk impacting in isolation, which given the strength of correlation seems unlikely.

For anyone seeking reassurance that the present framework equips us well, any objective analysis of the underlying causes and impact of the 2008 global crash would make grim reading. In fact, far from helping us confront these challenges, our present financial system seems more likely to simply magnify their effect.

As we have seen, at times of crisis fear and herd instinct subsume rational analysis and markets exhibit dangerously high levels of volatility. More damagingly, the whole ethos of our economic system is the continued delivery of economic growth, itself an agent of increasing levels of consumption, and in conjunction with population growth an exacerbant of many of the risks outlined above (more on which in section 5).

I draw the following conclusions from this:

1) Few of the significant risks that now confront us fit comfortably into our present risk assessment framework
2) That the impact of many of them will be felt over the next hundred years seems far more likely than not. Some, indeed, are impacting already
3) The financial impact of each is uncertain, but is likely to be profound
4) Not only are our present economic and financial systems not robust enough to withstand the fallout, they will also act to exacerbate its impact

Add into the mix some of the less familiar risks omitted from the list (for example a repeat of the 1859 Carrington event, an electrical storm which had only modest impact at the time but which could plunge the Western world into months of darkness if it were to happen today, or an event similar to the 1908 Tunguska incident, but in a geographic location or on a scale that wreaks considerably more havoc), and the notion that we as actuaries are in a position to quantify the financial impact of the significant risks that we now face begins to look fanciful indeed. While some Government ministers can be quick to recognise a one-in-1000 year flood event when they see one, presumably in the hope that they will have found alternative employment before their judgement is found wanting, it would be a particularly brave or foolish actuary who followed suit.

As a Profession that has an obligation to serve the public interest, that is keen to promote its risk management credentials and which purports to take a long term view, ought we not to be reflecting on how we can most effectively respond to the threat such unpredictable risks pose to our collective long term interests?

Clearly as individuals or as a Profession it is not uniquely in our gift to find and impose solutions to all these challenges, any more than it is in anyone else's. But neither does that mean it is appropriate for us to ignore them. In some instances the incidence of these risks lies beyond anyone's influence, but limiting the severity of their impact does not, and if recent history has taught us anything it is surely how ineffective Government often is at dispensing the art of risk management on our behalf. Looking to the future, it is clear to me if not to you that Government's response to some of these threats has to date been inadequate, and that is a public interest issue that ought to be of concern to us all.

It is not difficult to identify reasons why Government might struggle to provide the kind of leadership we now need. Governments don't like to be the harbingers of bad news, and regrettably not without some justification Government sees talk of hardship and personal sacrifice as a vote loser. It may also be that representatives of Government struggle to take a longer term view than anyone else does, a form of myopia that the demands of our short-term electoral cycle serve only to reinforce.

In the aftermath of the present crisis, while it is true that there is now general acceptance, both within and outside Government, of the fact that we face a period of relative *financial* austerity, that is only because the dreadful state of the public finances has made it impossible to deny (though that didn't stop some trying, for a while). There is still, however, precious little discussion of the kind of austerity our society really needs now to be embracing, austerity that relates to tough *lifestyle* choices, not financial ones.

At the heart of this grand failure of policy sits the dysfunctional relationship those in a position of influence (Government, us and others) have with the economic system that is meant to be serving us. It is handled as a temperamental child with kid gloves, its whims indulged, its nerves soothed for fear of the tantrums it might throw, its good moods a cause of joy for all and its depressions a source of national angst.

Yet if it is to have any hope of surviving all that reality is someday soon going to throw at it, we need our economic child to grow up fast. The time to take the tantrums and deal with them is now: the alternative is storing up trouble, for the moods are going to get worse and one day our delinquent economy might just bring the rest of its doting, extended family down with it.

Who is going to tell the parents? *Who is to make wise those who are required to have wisdom?*

Of Economics and Science

An exposition of all the arguments for and against the classification of economics as a science is not central to this paper's purpose, but given the nature and scale of its present doctrine of choice's recent failings, the question is nevertheless worth a little reflection.

Personally, I take a simplistic view of the question. I am happy to see the science net cast wide enough to encompass any discipline where theory can be reliably used to give structure to observation, and where experiment can be reliably used to test theory.

On that basis, I still consider economics to be more art than science.

If economics did have the credentials of a science, then one could argue that our present economic model is perhaps its greatest, and perhaps longest running, experiment. What conclusions can we draw from the results of that experiment to date?

While my own study of science may now be little more than a distant memory, I recall enough of the basics to believe that our modern economic system is one experiment that has been allowed to run long after the date at which any self-respecting scientist would have called time on it.

For scientists are sticklers for experimental detail. Measurement is all, and when the error term breaches their materiality threshold they know it is time to look for a better model.

No such constrains, however, for our long-running experiment in free market Capitalism. No scientist will be invited to call time on it, and the experiment has the ominous feel of a chain reaction that, if it were allowed to, could burn until its last drop of fuel is spent.

A full exploration of the flaws in conventional economic theory is worthy of a book on its own, and as it is a subject about which plenty has already been written I don't propose to examine it in great detail here. But there are certain basic weaknesses that I do need to touch upon, because they are relevant to this paper's central premise.

'Intangibles' seems as good a place to start as any.

Economists are familiar with intangibles. To the economist, intangibles are essentially the assets of a business that can't be seen, touched or physically measured. The accounting practice of placing value on intangible assets in company balance sheets is traditionally, and not unreasonably, legitimised and measured in terms of whatever somebody else is prepared to pay for them.

What you don't often hear economists and accountants talk about is intangible *liabilities,* which to those not versed in accountancy's darker arts might sound like a recipe for an imbalanced balance sheet.

But the problems really start when one looks beyond the corporate, to the balance sheet of UK plc and beyond. At this level, our balance sheet is full of intangibles, the vast majority of them liabilities. Intangible inter-generational debt, the intangible cost of environmental degradation, the intangible opportunity cost of consuming finite resources, etc. Only when viewed at this level does the scale of the hole sitting at the heart of our present economic model become fully apparent.

Unfortunately, the degree of rigour that is brought to bear in our approach to governance and accounting at corporate level is sadly lacking where it matters most, at the level of UK Plc. Business has little interest in this view, other than as a portent of the potential for market growth, and Governments have a pervasive tendency to discount or ignore liabilities (intangible or otherwise) that lie beyond their own event horizon (which often seems to extend little beyond the next big date in the electoral cycle).

This is a chronic systemic weakness, one whose consequences are only just beginning to be properly felt.

In short, our present economic doctrine is a failed experiment, one whose error term is swamping its objective, and whose terms of reference are drawn on timescales too short to render it fit for purpose. Or if you prefer soundbites, our present economic doctrine is perhaps in need of a little more focus on the 'eco' and a little less focus on the 'nomics'.

Parallels with Physics

The evolution of modern economics, and in particular of the financial markets that support them, is not without its parallels in science. However, for those who seek to bring order to economic chaos, they are not particularly reassuring ones.

In the field of physics, Newton's original deterministic model based on predictive physical laws held sway for many years, until the dark secrets of the quantum world were revealed to a disbelieving scientific community and a probabilistic view of reality emerged. Over time the currency of that probabilistic model has grown to the point where its validity is now universally accepted, but more recent developments in chaos theory, popularised by the so-called Butterfly Effect, go some way towards explaining why we are still unable to use that probabilistic view in any meaningful way to predict large-scale events in the real world. That small-scale events can beget unpredictable, large-scale consequences is either one of life's great joys or one of its worst nightmares, depending on whether you happen to be busy living it or trying to model it.

In the financial world, our own quantum revolution came with improvements in technology that allowed the development of more sophisticated stochastic modelling tools. These replaced our deterministic calculations with probabilistic, scenario-based projections as a more reliable basis for quantifying risks and their potential financial impact.

However, just as in the physical world, economic butterflies in our modern-day financial world are exposing the limitations of even a probabilistic approach to financial modelling. When markets so choose, good news is ignored; when markets so choose, bad news is ignored. The difference between the two can turn on the butterflies in an investor's stomach.

The result is that unpredictability is becoming an increasingly predominant characteristic of the system, and just as in the real world the result can be a storm that wreaks havoc. And in another curious parallel with the real World, the intensity of some of those storms appears to be growing.

The profound effect that human psychology can have on financial markets is nothing new. Galbraith wrote about it at length in his analysis of the 1929 crash, it found notable incarnations long before that in the form of Dutch tulips and the South Sea Bubble, and a review of the history books would reveal numerous less spectacularly vertiginous departures from market fundamentals in between.

What is notable, however, is that a number of features of our modern global economy are now combining, in what one might see as the financial equivalent of global warming, to magnify the impact these human 'butterflies' can have on financial markets.

Consider, for example, the following influences:

- Improvements in technology that have facilitated the instant flow of capital and information around the globe and led to an explosion in real-time trading
- The globalisation of financial markets, strengthening ties and financial dependencies between markets in different countries
- A shift in emphasis in the sourcing of profit, away from long term investment and towards short term trading activity
- An explosion in hedge funds and other private investment vehicles, whose sole activity is short-term trading, accentuating this trend
- An increase in technology-driven, rule-based trading
- Greater resultant short-term volatility in prices, itself a reinforcer of short term trading activity
- A proliferation in the range and complexity of financial products that has reduced the transparency of financial markets and made management of financial risks more challenging, more time-consuming and less reliable.

Does this combination of factors not create a climate where reason more easily falls victim to market forces and chaos more easily permeates the system? That seems to be what we are witnessing.

It does not help that we are also entering an age of increasing global uncertainty. Unless remedial steps are taken to address some of the exacerbants above, the financial storms of the future may well intensify further, to the point where the financial system itself might collapse. As indeed it came uncomfortably close to doing last year.

In short, without reform of financial markets the crash of 2008 may soon look anything but the outlier we'd all like to believe it is.

A good place to start tackling the issue might be to begin reining in some of the activities that are exacerbating this volatility. In which respect some of those who lead our industry's instinctive opposition to any initiatives aimed at containing the excesses of our modern day financial system is depressingly familiar in its short-sightedness, as indeed is Government acquiescence to their threats and tired arguments.

Does the Profession have a view on this matter of considerable public interest?

Capital Punishment

As AIG and no small number of banks can painfully attest to, nowhere is this new economic reality impacting more profoundly than in the balance sheets of financial services institutions.

As has already been said by a good few Politicians with an interest, the World's economy in 2008 entered uncharted waters. Quite what the long term consequence will be for our traditional role as actuaries remains to be seen, but that impact is already being felt.

In January 2009 I attended the presentation and discussion, at Staple Inn, of Bernard Bergman's paper, 'Capital – It's Over-rated!'. A lively discussion followed Bernhard's presentation, but none of the participants noted the presence of the elephant in the capital requirements room: nobody questioned how legitimate an actuary's assessment of capital requirements might actually be in present circumstances.

I pose that question not to undermine our role as actuaries – I cannot think of any other Profession that is any better placed to exercise such judgement - but to highlight a trap that as career analysts we are sometimes predisposed to falling into, namely placing too much emphasis on the theory of financial modelling and giving inadequate consideration to the limits of its practical application. When one is used to analysing trees, it is sometimes easy to lose sight of the wood.

Across the Pond, among others there must have been one or two AIG actuaries who were feeling the heat of financial crisis last year at quarters that were a little too close for comfort. While for the time being a degree of sanity seems to have been restored to financial markets, it would be naive for us to assume that something similar could not happen over here.

If it did, should a UK-based insurer fail all eyes will inevitably turn to its last risk report, and in the circumstances we should expect any protestations after the event about the efficacy of a 1-in-200 year event capital assessment model, or the challenges of sensibly populating it, to garner little sympathy.

It seems to me that one of the biggest risks we are running is with our risk model itself. If one accepts this, then as a Profession we face a choice: do we highlight our concerns now as a collective, do we leave it for the first actuary that gets caught out to fight his own corner, or do we hope that if and when the risk model does fail that it is on such a scale that the Profession will not be seen as culpable?

If this is to be another subject about which the Profession is to maintain its traditional diplomatic silence, it ought to be on the basis of sound reasoning rather than expediency. The limiting factor, after all, is not one of actuarial ability but systemic weakness. There would be no shame in admitting that, and some might even consider it the Profession's duty to do so.

Economic Uncertainty

Any financial model that had predicted at the beginning of 2008 that the share prices of some high street banks would shed 80% or more of their value, or that the dollar would rise 50% against the pound, or that oil prices would double then fall by 70% before the end of the year would have been dismissed as fundamentally flawed. Such statistics are a graphic and sobering manifestation of the nature of the underlying forces to which our modern economy can be subjected.

If more businesses are failing today than ever before – and they are – it is surely not for lack of access to appropriate financial management tools. Actuaries of the past would look on in envious awe at the range and sophistication of the financial models now at our disposal. But in truth the sophistication of those models has long since ceased to be our limiting factor.

Which leads to another curious if rather unscientific parallel with modern physics. I'm sure financial modelling couldn't have been further from Heisenberg's mind when he first conceived of his uncertainty principle, but it is nonetheless interesting and not a little ironic that as our financial models become ever more sophisticated so some of the assumptions with which we populate them are becoming ever less reliable.

Those observers who talk of a casino economy do a disservice to casinos. Casinos, governed as they are by the laws of probability, are an actuary's dream. Our modern economy and its chaotic financial system, by contrast, is surely far more the stuff of actuaries' nightmares.

As placing reliance upon past experience to inform future expectation is one of the cornerstones of our trade, perhaps it is time we asked ourselves whether it is not just Government that now finds itself in uncharted waters. As actuarial truths go that would be a particularly inconvenient one, but if it is to be dismissed, again it should do so on the basis of cold logic not expediency. At the very least this seems to be a subject worthy of more open and honest debate than it is presently attracting.

The Economics of Remuneration

Something of a taboo subject, perhaps, but in a paper such as this I would need a better excuse than that for failing to pass comment on it.

In fact there are two good reasons for considering it here.

The first is the belief, in the minds of a public now flush with armchair financial expertise, that remuneration policy in the Financial Services sector, particularly at the top end of the pay scale, has lost its moral compass in recent years (a view now neatly symbolised for a generation by the size of Fred Goodwin's pension).

The second is the value in exploring the impact that a flawed industry remuneration practices might have both on the career choices we make and on the efficacy with which actuaries our intellectual capital is deployed.

No small number of actuaries will at some point in their working lives have the pleasure of serving remuneration committees in one capacity or another. Indeed, spanning as we do pretty much all positions on the Financial Services remuneration spectrum, from actuarial trainees to Chief Executives of large banks and all stops in between, it could be argued that as a Profession we have something of a unique perspective on the subject.

Typically, remuneration for mainstream roles is set through a process of job evaluation, which assigns to each job a grade based on benchmarked evaluation against a range of different criteria. Salary bandings are attributed to each job grade, and a particular jobholder's position within that band is typically determined by past experience and their level of performance in post. In practice the peculiar dimensions of some actuarial roles often fit rather uncomfortably into the evaluation process, but with the right benchmarking the scale can usually be flexed enough to accommodate them.

All of which seems eminently logical until one digs a little deeper into the murky origins of the salary scale itself, down to the place where remuneration policy meets with the dark forces of 'the market'.

Nobody disputes conventional wisdom that overall benefits packages employers offer to their employees need to be broadly comparable with those of other companies in the same industry and locale if they are to be competitive. But how are the underlying benchmarks for different roles and for all such players actually being *set?*

How does one objectively decide whether a financial reporting actuary should be paid more or less than, for example, a Home Office pathologist, or a climate change scientist, or a Member of Parliament? These aren't questions we ever ask because they never seem relevant. Yet if we lived in a society that wanted to ensure that relative contribution was properly rewarded, such questions would be very relevant.

The obvious riposte is that we never need to ask because they are implicitly answered for us by market forces. For skilled roles, in generic terms this is expedited through the interaction of supply and demand for specialist skills, as influenced in particular by the following factors:

(i)	Based on individual predilections, how intrinsically attractive is that particular career choice relative to alternative career opportunities
(ii)	What time and effort would one need to invest in attaining the level of competence needed to successfully practice it
(iii)	What particular innate skills and attributes are required, and how scarce are they
(iv)	How valuable the end result is directly or indirectly perceived to be by society

In this view of the world, remuneration is the variable that brings these influencers of supply and demand into balance.

Clearly there is much about the market dynamic in relation to the supply of and demand for skilled labour that does work towards ensuring that a fair remunerative price is struck.

However, even a cursory review of the causes and fallout from the banking crisis is enough to reveal that there is also much that doesn't.

If we had an economic system that struck a better balance between the interests of short term profit and long term good in striking determining the relative worth of different career choices, this would be of less concern.

If we were living in an age when the opportunity cost of poorly-deployed intellectual capital did not have such profound consequence, it might also be of less concern.

Unfortunately, neither hypothesis is true.

In present circumstances, only for the World's poorest people should the acquisition of wealth be the main priority. For the rest of us – quite literally – there are more burning priorities.

The World may have many colours and the people in it many motivations, but the underlying truth is that it is in the culture of modern society for people *in general* to be seduced more by the attractions of acquiring wealth than the attractions of contributing to the greater good. If we are honest, as a Profession we would have to concede that we have hitherto done rather well out of our society's balance of priorities in that respect. As my own father so wryly observed many moons ago in response to his son's proposed choice of career; "few jobs pay as well as those that involve looking after other people's money".

It is society's current predilection for the acquisition of wealth that so often distorts the balance of (i) and (iv) above, and it is this predilection that was so instrumental in creating the situation that allowed some of those who run our banking industry to bring the World economy to its knees.

Whatever one's view of the successes and failures of Government – and what a landscape that is - leaving Government to defend the greater good while the rest of us pursue greater wealth is still an abdication of collective responsibility. Few would defend MPs conduct in the wake of the recent expenses scandal, yet while they have only themselves to blame for the media feeding frenzy that ensued, it still says something pretty unsavoury about the society they govern that so many of its citizens invest so much time and effort criticizing the morality of those who lead it and so little time reflecting on their own contribution to the moral failures of modern-day society as a whole. And yes, that includes our own Profession.

In the welter of recrimination that accompanied said scandal, few were minded to ask what kind of economic system finds equity in paying the same basic salary to someone who typically represents the interests of around 90,000 people as a Member of Parliament as it does to a newly qualified actuary, and less than a tenth of what someone can walk away with for ruining a bank.

As we have seen, rewards that many outside our industry regard as obscene are routinely defended by many of those with a vested interest on the inside on grounds that reining in the excess would risk a flight of talent. But what of the bigger question, namely what kind of global economic system allows people to be paid so much for this kind of contribution *anywhere?* The answer is one with distorted emphasis on the creation of financial wealth and the quest for short term profit.

Consequently, while it might be convenient for us as individuals to presume market efficacy will ensure that our remuneration policies reflect the true value of the activities that occupy our time, the flaws in our present socio-economic model often contrive to ensure that they don't.

We are in urgent need of a new social contract, one that promotes a better balance between short and long term objectives, between public interest and private enterprise and in the distribution of wealth. In the wake of the failings of our present model, the erosion in the public's trust of a wide range of institutions that purport to represent them has reached dangerously corrosive levels. While that problem has many facets, a fairer, more transparent reward system should be an essential component of any solution.

Regrettably, all the indications are that such a solution is still some way off. No amount of dysfunction in the market, it seems, will induce Government to regard interference in any aspect of the market remuneration dynamic as anything other than anathema. Instead, the problem is devolved to non-executive directors, shareholders and the regulator, who have neither the will (in the case of the first two) nor the mandate (in the case of the latter) to properly address it.

This is hardly the kind of gamekeeper response to strike fear into the hearts of the poachers. Likewise, while latterly shareholder criticism has indeed at times been more vocal, in the midst of a deep recession this is hardly surprising, and it is still proving largely ineffective. The truth is that until there is a cultural shift away from a finance-driven, instant gratification society towards one that values long term investment, shareholder scrutiny is destined to remain a weak form of governance, and to rely on it is a weak form of Government. As an ex-City man himself, Lord Myners, the Government appointee tasked with tackling the problem must surely know this, and it is disingenuous of him to infer otherwise.

However, that is not to absolve shareholders of their responsibility, and the fact is that much of the power to exercise that responsibility rests with institutional investors, the very organisations many of us work for. Unfortunately, while expecting the Board of one large financial institution to instruct its investment managers to take a tough line on the Boardroom excesses of others would not quite be the equivalent of turkeys voting for Christmas, neither is it something we should bank on (no pun intended).

That Board Directors (and investment managers) believe they have better things to be doing with their time than concerning themselves with such details is perhaps understandable, and not without some justification. For all the public's justifiable ire, excessive pay is still just a symptom of malaise, not one of its causes.

Yet financial sector excess remains fundamentally a far bigger problem than MPs expenses, and it remains a huge issue in the public psyche, with each new revelation adding a little more steam to a public kettle that has yet to be given an outlet.

Where, in the circumstances, might the public reasonably look for some influence to be brought to bear?

Our Profession plays a key role in the management of financial institutions, and our Profession is passionate about matters of public interest, so where is its policy position on this key issue of public concern? It is a subject about which the Profession's independent view could carry some weight, and if it had something constructive to say could do much to enhance its public profile. Does the Profession agree with Lord Myners, that institutional shareholders should be doing more to rein in excess, and how would it propose that this might best be achieved?

Perhaps the Profession feel that it has too many people in its ranks who would not wish it to pass comment. Before his conversion from poacher to gamekeeper it would have been difficult to imagine a James Crosby supporting initiatives aimed at constraining excessive remuneration. Which thought raises an interesting question: how many James Crosbys would the Profession need in its ranks to maintain its silence on a subject such as this?

Not as many as it needed to stifle its merger plans, I would wager. Yet while the Profession's stated strategic priority is to support its members' interests in their various guises, should not the public interest take precedence when the two are in conflict?

Many a balanced perspective can find itself distorted by convenience. Does the Profession recognise the conflict of interest this issue presents it with? Like the merger, outcome, this has the feel of a situation where the wider public interest is being held hostage to the interests of a minority of the Profession's membership.

In the meantime, the degree of mismatch between the respective objectives of pursuit of a greater good and pursuit of a greater bank balance, and the extent to which as a society we so often seem to favour the latter over the former, continues its corrosive work. Fortunately for those who exploit the gap, and helping to spare the blushes of those who govern us, it is a mismatch that even an actuary would struggle to put a price on.

Whatever our Profession's position on the subject, one does not need to be an actuary to understand that some of those in the higher echelons of the Financial Services industry are remunerated more generously than their contribution to society warrants, and that some of them have latterly been incentivised to act in ways that are detrimental to the long term public interest.

To be fair, it is a problem not confined to our own industry. In a year when the FTSE 100 lost nearly one third of its value, we discover that executive salaries increased by an average of around 10%[5]. When the rationale for this is challenged, the typical response is that salaries are meant to reflect a long term view.

Well, here is a good measure of the long term view: over the last thirty years, CEO pay has typically trebled relative to average employee remuneration, and the gap is continuing to widen. This might be easier to justify if their companies had brought similar benefit to wider society, but at the end of 2008 the FTSE 100 was back at 1997 levels.

Cue the next defence: Executive pay must be maintained at competitive levels, or there will be a flight of talent. In times of economic prosperity companies have been able to apply this principle year-in, year-out without much scrutiny. Benchmarks are set by the market, and companies must remain competitive. Case closed.

When times are harder, as we have witnessed in the wake of the present crisis, the issue tends to get escalated and the debate goes national. But unfortunately the debate hasn't tended to become any more well-informed. Instead the same arguments against change continue to be advanced, but on a national scale. It is important that the UK remains competitive, we are told; we must offer the best packages to attract and retain the best people.

Thus is the uncomfortable question of why pay awards to senior executives always seem to outstrip everyone else's consistently and conveniently sidestepped. It's just 'the market'. Some other company, or some other country sets the bar. Delete as appropriate.

Into the Executive pay mix we should add another interesting and topical ingredient. Boardrooms, it seems, along with some golf clubs and the Banking industry, remain one of the last strong bastions of sexual inequality. Males still outnumber females as Executives around FTSE 100 Boardroom tables by fifteen to one, and their packages outstrip their female counterparts by an average of 60% [5].

Another statistic: a recent Leeds University Business School study by Professor Nick Wilson revealed that substituting just one set of testosterone-pumping Y chromosomes around the Boardroom table with those of the fairer sex reduces the probability of company insolvency by around 20%.

I draw three conclusions from this: (i) executive pay is too high (lest we feel too sorry for the 1 in 15, at the end of 2008 the lack of a Y chromosome was still worth an average salary of £1.3m in FTSE 100 Boardrooms); (ii) there is sex inequality in the Boardroom, in terms of both the proportion of women and their relative remuneration; and (iii) evidence suggests that it would be in the interests of sound governance and corporate stability for there to be more.

All of which hints at a rather obvious solution to Boardroom excess. Indeed rarely can so many birds have been at the mercy of just one stone. Unfortunately, whatever the benefits doubts must remain about whether our male-dominated remuneration committees would be willing to strike a blow for sex equality and vote for application of the current female scale to all Board Executives, or whether our male-dominated Government would want them to, given how many of its members have a habit of slipping quietly into Directorships themselves as soon as they've left office.

Less doubt, however, about what our slightly less male-dominated Profession might have to say on the subject. Not a lot. *Actuaries Don't Do Executive remuneration*, perhaps, in the same way that *Actuaries Don't Do Banking*.

Actuaries don't do golf either, as a Profession, but there are plenty who dabble with it as individuals, and therein perhaps lies the rub: actuaries dabble in many things that their Profession chooses not to comment on. Unlike golf, however, many of them are also matters of considerable public interest.

I digress. More generally and more pertinently, there is enough evidence to the contrary for it to be foolish for us to try and pretend that as actuaries our professional training and moral backbone places us beyond the influence of flawed remuneration practices. The propensity of people to be motivated by money, and to make career choices and management decisions based largely around acquiring it, is familiar to all of us, if not when we look in the mirror then when we look at what motivates some of our Professional colleagues.

While the Profession is hardly in a strong position to wield great influence over the market dynamic of Financial Services industry remuneration even if it was minded to, I do think it is incumbent upon us as members of a Profession that places the public interest at the heart of all that it does to at least be aware of the limitations of present practice, and on occasion to ask more searching questions about the worth of some of the activities for which we find ourselves rewarded. Furthermore, given that we all now have a better understanding of just how disastrous an impact flawed remuneration policies can have on the public interest, I also think the Profession should be doing more to ensure that its members do not contribute to the problem – a subject I return to in section 10.

Above all, we should be mindful of the perceptions we create as a Profession. We operate in an industry whose widely-discredited top-end remuneration structures are seen as having contributed to the present financial crisis. Yet our passion as a Profession to identify public interest issues where our input might be of benefit to society hasn't, as yet, extended to commenting upon one that we have a close interest in.

While in the circumstances that may be understandable, in the eyes of a sceptical public it will also look distinctly convenient, and avoiding the issue hardly sits comfortably with the Profession's attempts to promote its public interest credentials.

The Psychology of Wealth

I am always struck by how often, and in how many different contexts, the 80/20 rule seems to be a good proxy for reality. There is one measure, however, that has long since left the 80/20 rule behind.

To the uninitiated, a World in which 20% of the people shared 80% of the wealth might be considered an unduly polarised one. What word, then, to describe a World in which 1% of the people control 40% of the wealth? [6]

Many spring to mind, but neither 'fair' nor 'stable' would be among them. Yet this is our present reality.

It can be difficult for those of us not so driven to comprehend what motivates people who already have wealth way beyond the dreams of most to spend so much of their time trying to accumulate more. Is it ego? Is it insecurity? Is it just financial megalomania?

However many and varied the reasons might be for their behaviour, it is perhaps enough simply that we recognise their type and recognise how little regard they often have for the interests of the rest of us in their quest. Protestations that they are 'creating wealth for us all' need to be viewed critically in the context of the above statistics and the events of the last twelve months.

Of course these people and their apologists will protest that their endeavours are good for the economy, and ergo good for all of us. Yet in truth the activities of only a small number of them contribute to *real* economic growth, and many of the rest – the few that turn philanthropist excepted – often end up exploiting rather more people than they help.

Perhaps a little harshly given the increase in tax revenues, but with some justification given the continuing polarisation in the distribution of wealth and the role our industry has played in it, few members of the public have been left feeling that they have gained any appreciable benefit from the boom in Financial Services over the last two decades. That number seems likely to drop further in the coming years as the cost of the industry's recent follies eats increasingly into the public purse.

Yet when it comes to incentivising those who lead the way, the generally-accepted view still seems to be that a) to attract the best people, you have to offer the best packages, and b) if you don't offer the best packages, the best people will up sticks and go where the best packages are offered.

Without wishing to sound cynical, this could also be seen as a very convenient argument on the part of those who stand to gain from said bidding war, especially given that it is this same cabal of people who seem to be its most vociferous proponents.

There are a number of reasons to suggest that it is time those who peddle this notion's bluff was called:

- It is now abundantly clear that some of those who were judged to be the 'best people' were anything but
- It is also clear that the link between such packages and the drive to achieve growth in profits can lead people to take reckless risks
- This policy may not always attract the best people, but it will always attract the greediest
- It is far from clear why, as a matter of principle, anyone would think that the kind of people who would choose to leave Britain's shores at the drop of a hat for the sole purpose of pursuing greater wealth elsewhere are best placed to promote the long term interests of the British public
- We are entering an age when, in the name of progress, our industry leaders will need to be concerning themselves with an increasing number of factors beyond the purely financial. Those who are conditioned to be motivated only by profit and bonus may struggle to adapt, and will almost certainly not be the best people for the task

Only fear and vested interests stand in the way of progress on this issue. Indeed the former is the only effective weapon still wielded by the latter to obstruct it, all rational argument long since having capitulated to events and all reasoned debate having found itself sabotaged as a result.

On the face of it, a Profession with an independent view, a penchant for analysis and an in-depth understanding of risk ought to be well placed to counter such obfuscation. Indeed, add in our Profession's public interest mandate and one could put together a convincing case to say that we are obligated to do so. Yet it is far from apparent, looking at our own current priorities and agenda, that the Actuarial Profession is not presently seeing the World through equally distorted eyes.

Having observed our industry for many years from the inside and at close quarters, I predict that when some future Government does conquer its paranoia, does recognise that much of what passes for 'investment activity' in today's Financial Services industry is indeed – to quote Lord Turner - 'socially useless', and does eventually act to restore some degree of sanity to pay packages at the top end of the industry, there will be no mass exodus of talent that is critical to the prosperity of the British economy.

It seems unlikely, however, that there would be any appreciable exodus of those responsible for promulgating that myth either. Which in at least one respect is regrettable, because only when the industry has largely cleansed itself of people who think in this way will it be in a position to rebuild its reputation, rediscover its core purpose and values, re-evaluate its priorities and activities based on their long term benefit to society not their short term benefit to the bank accounts of those who govern it, and embrace the kind of reforms that are necessary both for the industry's long term good and for everyone else's. And who knows, we might then even begin to see something closer to sex equality in the Boardroom.

A reduction in Executive packages at the top end of the scale would at least weed out some of those whose allegiance to Britain is based solely on fickle financial self-interest, and the move to more balanced remuneration policy would help to remove one of the obstacles to market efficiency, in particular with regard to the role discussed earlier that distorted pay incentives play in promoting the inefficient deployment of intellectual capital.

Despite limited tangible progress to date, I am optimistic that industry remuneration policy may soon start heading in the right direction. Society's notion of what is valuable is in the process of undergoing a shift of seismic proportions, as people are beginning to understand that no amount of money will spare them, and more pertinently their descendants, from a collective fate whose agents have no financial currency and no respect for financial markets. As the constraints of earthly reality begin to bite, this change in sentiment will gather momentum. In its wake, the reputations of those who continue to defend the indefensible will quickly crumble - as indeed the reputations of those who defend the top end of our industry's present remuneration packages already have.

In which respect the Profession should beware. Only in benign times does the acquiescence of those with an interest pass unnoticed, and the years ahead are going to be anything but benign. If our Profession does not soon start to walk the talk or put some meat on the bones of its public interest rhetoric (pick your own cliché) it should prepare itself for a bleak future.

6.   The Growth Delusion

While economics may have its limitations as a science, that didn't stop New Scientist running an issue leading on the subject last October (The Folly of Growth [7]). If the title itself isn't enough to put you off, their selection of articles is worth a read.

As actuaries the concept of growth is not just familiar to us. So routinely and for so long have we factored it into our business plans, investment assumptions and financial projections that it has become one of the paradigms of our trade.

At a time when our Government is using every financial trick at its disposal to try and kick growth back into our stalled economy, however, it is a sobering thought that the World would need to lose around two thirds of its population to sustainably support the average Briton's present standard of living across the globe.

We can safely say that nobody will be volunteering. In the meantime, the World's population still continues to grow and the Pope still rails against birth control (though interestingly enough even *he's* now calling for a new socio-economic model and a revised set of priorities).

Another sobering statistic, and one of the famous 80/20 rule's less comforting global incarnations: around 20% of the World's population are responsible for 80% of its consumption.

Against this backdrop, no great insight is required to see that it is the paradigm of growth itself that is in need of challenging. Yet curiously, when it comes to this particular question, insight from those in authority – not to say some in our own Profession - seems to be in particularly short supply.

No actuarial training is needed to understand that, on a planet with finite resources and an ever-growing population, an economic model whose measure of success relies upon ever-increasing levels of prosperity and consumption is fundamentally flawed. Yet this is still the only language that our business leaders and most of our politicians seem able to speak.

It is in the long term interests of all that a better, more sustainable solution is found, so why is the Profession not lending its own voice to those of religious leaders, the Sustainable Development Group, and any number of scientists and progressive thinkers in challenging this doctrine?

A sceptic looking in from outside the Profession might conclude that sensitivity to commercial interests may be stifling debate. A cynic might conclude that it is the Profession's own interests that are stifling debate. As an actuary, I wonder whether the Profession considers that it has invested too much of its own recent history in the concept of growth to now be seen questioning it.

If the Emperor of Growth's nudity were merely an embarrassment, to ignore it might be good politic. But it isn't. Our emperor's taste in clothing is in the process of extracting a heavy price. As such it is a subject worthy of far more discussion within the Profession and elsewhere than it presently seems to attract. Thus the reason I seek to explore the concept in more detail here.

Growth in its different guises is a perennial feature of our actuarial assumption sets, where it is reflected in year-on-year increases in sales and profit. We also use it in our investment assumptions, in setting long term rates of return, and it is an integral component of the discount rates that we traditionally use to value future cash flows and profit.

It has not been our tradition to question the *principle* of growth as expressed in these different ways. Such debate as there is usually revolves around what values it might be appropriate to assign to the different measures of growth we use in practice. For that purpose we variously rely on the corporate view, market perception or current real yields on long term investments depending on the nature and purpose of the particular growth factor in question. Usually, provided the assumptions made aren't significantly out of line with those typically used elsewhere nobody is unduly concerned.

But why do we place such trust in the principle of growth, and why do we place such trust in the market to inform it when markets increasingly seem so fickle and unreliable a guide to so much else?

The answer, perhaps, is that the experience of recent history has broadly supported the use of a market-based approach.

But what if the past is no longer a guide to the future? What if a fundamental sea-change in ideological thinking is imminent?

While that may seem an unlikely notion to many, it would be dangerous to dismiss it. For while the public may not yet be showing much appetite at an individual level to embrace the kind of changes that will be needed to avoid - or at least to some degree mitigate – the scale of trouble that lies ahead, people are at least becoming increasingly aware that trouble is our destination, and that a quick return to increasing consumption and growth is simply going to get us all there quicker.

It is perhaps time, then, that the principle of economic growth was subjected to a little more scrutiny.

The Nature of Growth

The next time you factor a real rate of return into a long term financial projection, try not to do it on autopilot. Instead ask yourself what that growth represents, where it is likely to come from, and what the longer term consequences of delivering it might be.

A difficult questions to answer, perhaps, but as insurance companies and pension funds are custodians of so significant a fraction of UK Plc's investment portfolio it is not one we can afford to ignore.

Does the growth you are assuming rely on increasing our already large debt to future generations? Does it rely on increasing consumption of the Earth's natural resources? Is it to be fuelled more by borrowing and optimism than by innovation?

If we were asking these questions retrospectively of the growth we witnessed during the boom that preceded the latest bust, the answer would be 'yes' to all three, and little has thus far changed to suggest that the answer will be any different next time around.

At the time of writing, over one third of the FTSE 100 index by value relies directly on extracting raw materials from the Earth. Much of the rest relies directly or indirectly on a continuing flow of cheap goods, cheap labour or both. Neither are durable agents of growth.

Not all growth is unsustainable, of course: innovation, improvements in technology and being more efficient about how we do things are all laudable. But at some point the law of diminishing returns has to kick in, and we should be mindful of the limited contribution these factors are now making to the *overall* growth that we see or assume in our projections.

In a wider context, the post-globalised World has thus far been kind to Britain, providing a flow of cheap goods, cheap labour and cheap money to sustain what our dwindling manufacturing base could not. But times are changing: the oil that has helped sustain the UK economy is running out: the transient relief of today's low interest rates cannot disguise the fact that the days of cheap money are gone: the recent drop in sterling has shown that when things turn sour money can leave rather more quickly than it arrived: the flow of cheap goods and labour has stalled, and it cannot flow forever.

Why would our Profession not wish to bring its vision, analytical skills and risk management expertise to bear on highlighting the growth problem, and finding a more sustainable solution to it? Do our public interest commitments not create an obligation for us to do so? Why is it that New Scientist has so much more to say on this subject than we do, when it is so peripheral to their raison d'etre yet so central to ours?

Perhaps a clue to the answer lies in the last question. When as a Profession are we going to be bold enough – or honest enough – to admit that the continuing quest for economic growth is proving detrimental to the long term interest on the grandest of scales?

While greed and optimism are both enemies of reason, when it comes to challenging the paradigm of growth fear is the real killer. Fear plucks impotence from virtue, fear corrodes conviction, fear flays fortitude, fear drives people into herds and fear makes Governments weak when we need them to be strong.

In the hands of those with influence, fear can be a potent weapon. Witness how it has been used by those with a vested interest, not just by apologists for industry excess but by lobby groups, IT consultants, the Government, our security services and so on to influence public opinion by exaggerating threats from, for example, the Millennium bug ('it could bring down the global economy') to capping bankers bonuses ('it will hurt the City and the UK economy') to the foxhunting ban ('a devastating blow to the rural economy') to the terrorist threat ('we're at War').

By contrast, the threats that *really* ought to scare us - those listed in section 5 – tend to be played down, impotence and fear of consequence combining to render those who lead us incapable of confronting them and the rest of us preferring not to contemplate them.

Perhaps what most keeps the paradigm of growth alive, despite all the evidence accumulating of the long term damage it is inflicting, is the fear of the wealthy and those who lead us of what might replace it. Without growth what is left? In the absence of an unlikely lottery win, only the prospect of growth (or lottery wins) feeds the aspirations of so many for the lifestyle of so few; without growth there is only redistribution, a society of winners and losers where he who grabs more leaves someone else with less. And few who have done rather well out of the growth model themselves are going to relish selling a message like that to the electorate, in any circumstance.

The only solution I can see that offers the hope of a stabe transition is for us as a society to find a mode of existence that demotes the overzealous quest for material wealth, in all its guises, to a more fitting position in the league table of our aspirations. That will require leadership of a kind that we have not yet had an opportunity to experience.

One of two things will eventually break the present impasse. One is in our collective gift to exercise, and the other will be a consequence of not doing so. Will the pre-emptive application of cool reason win out, or shall we simply wait for the impact of harsh reality? Before choosing the latter we should consider first the risk that consequence might by then lie well beyond our influence.

Risk-aversion is a trait that as actuaries we often stand accused of, but I consider this to be a little unfair. Not because we aren't, but because there is a good case to be made that risk aversion is a symptom of the human condition. Looking at recent events in the banking industry one could be forgiven for thinking otherwise, but gambling for personal gain with loaded dice and other people's money is hardly a fair test on which to base such a judgement. The simple fact is that for much of the time risk aversion, in the form of fear of failure, dictates many decisions made by many people in many walks of life. In that respect, as actuaries we are not so different.

The paradox is that what appear to be – indeed often are – low risk decisions for individuals can turn out to be high risk when adopted in the collective. Investment managers keep a watchful eye on the competition and manage portfolios that track falling indices and underperforming sectors in the process: wise heads employed by not so wise banks take the safe option and say nothing of reckless risks for fear of persecution: those who saw an economic bubble ready for bursting kept quiet, out of fear of being wrong or fear of being seen holding the pin. Conformity is seen as the best form of self-protection. If you're going to fail, do it in numbers; the alternative could jeopardise your career.

The key lesson – one that our Profession's present strategy suggests it may still have to learn - is that if big threats aren't addressed in the collective, they can easily end up not being addressed at all.

The paradigm of growth represents just such a threat. It perpetuates for fear of the alternative. Few individuals critique it, particularly and perhaps understandably those who are mindful of offending the commercial sensitivities of those upon whose continuing support they presume their own career progression might depend.

For that reason, any effective challenge to the paradigm of growth will need to be a collective challenge. The reason I believe that we as a Profession should be mounting one is simple: we are living in fear of the wrong alternative. While a life of constrained growth might well prove more painful in the short term, a life without constraints on growth will certainly prove a lot more painful in the long term.

Ours wouldn't be the first society that collapsed under the weight of its own ambitions. The history books are littered with them, each with its own cautionary tale to tell. But what will set the next collapse apart, should it come to pass, will surely be the nature and scale of its impact.

Are we a Profession that takes a long term view, or not? Does the Profession believe that the unwavering pursuit of economic growth makes this collapse more likely, or not?

The Grand Illusion

When one sees growth in this more searching light, not only does its profile change but the contribution made by our own industry is also thrown into starker contrast. In a World that valued growth only if it was real and sustainable, much of the recent expansion in our own industry would join rising house prices and increasing levels of debt as one of growth's false prophets.

For in essence, while the Financial Services industry plays a big part in the deployment, manipulation and redistribution of wealth, its role in the *creation* of wealth is seen to be minimal.

That so few think about our industry in these terms, and that those in the higher echelons of its rank continue to be paid so well, is testimony to the power of illusion to the contrary. Many, it seems - including our own Government - have been seduced into thinking that the Financial Services industry is a far more important contributor to the welfare and development of our society than it actually is.

In a wider socio-economic context, it is an act of great folly that growth has become so central a measure of our success, and an act of equally great folly that considerations of sustainability have still to be factored into it. Moreover while there are plenty of alternative, and increasingly more appropriate, benchmarks of human progress – some of which I touch upon in the last section of this paper - unfortunately our present economic model of choice has no mechanism for placing proper value on them.

The great challenge for our Profession, our industry, our Government and others is that our present economic model has played so central a role in the recent evolution of each that to relinquish any of its tenets, or even to concede its failings, is seen by many as unthinkable. Thus does a collective state of denial continue to prevail.

The strength of this illusion in the UK has been reinforced by the growth of London as a financial centre, but if one views that from a global perspective and against the backdrop of recent events, this too is revealed to be another false prophet. The growth of London as a financial centre had little to do with sustainable development and much to do with London having sucked in capital investment and resource from around the World. As we have witnessed over the last twelve months in the form of a falling exchange rate and crashing commercial property values, when circumstances change that investment can disappear as quickly as it arrived.

It was not just Government that gained from perpetuating the idea that the growth we were witnessing in the Financial Services sector was anything other than real and sustainable. Plenty in our own industry have benefited considerably from that perception too, and many continue to do so. In which respect it has almost certainly been to our industry's advantage that the same level of rigour that is applied at corporate level to monitoring the performance of our individual businesses these days is not brought to bear in monitoring the performance of the Financial Services industry as a whole.

At corporate level we have more management information than ever before. Our companies are awash with it. Our Boards obsess about it, and rightly so (though whether they always use it effectively or always ask the right questions of it is another matter). Yet if one asked simple questions about performance of the insurance sector as a whole, or the banking sector as a whole, answers are harder to come by.

For example what is the trend in the number each has employed over the last twenty years? At what average cost? How has the ratio of Board remuneration to average employee remuneration changed? What *real* aggregate returns have been achieved in each of these years on funds invested? How does that split between private equity, hedge funds and institutional investment? What was the total number of customers? What was the total amount invested? What is the trend in average industry cost per customer? What is the trend in annual reported profit per customer and per employee for different industry segments? What is the split of profit by activity? What is the trend in the ratio of company pension contributions (split between defined benefit and defined contribution schemes) to profit across FTSE 100 companies, and across industry sectors? To what extent might the answers to such questions and others shed light on other recently-published findings, that the distribution of wealth in Britain is becoming more polarised than ever, and the tax burden is falling disproportionately on individuals rather than corporations and on the less well-off rather than the wealthy?

It might be instructive to explore the reasons for the disparity in the quality of information available to Boards when running their companies compared with that used by successive Governments to run the country, but it is not in the scope of this paper to do so.

I will, though, offer a view as to what story that information might tell.

In general, I think it would show that the people who have collectively benefited *most* by the explosion in the Financial Services sector are those who are employed by it, not those who buy its products and services; it would show that the private equity and hedge fund investors' gain has been the institutional and pension fund investors' loss; it would show that customers are less satisfied with the service they are getting; it would reveal the degree to which pension fund benefits have in general been eroded, and the degree to which deficits could have been reduced by better funding in the boom years; it would show the extent to which profit is mismatched with both risk and the social value of the activity that generates it; it would show that advances in technology have not yielded equivalent advances in efficiency; and it would show that the industry as a whole has been a principal agent in polarising the distribution of wealth.

I would like to be proved wrong. If anyone has reliable data that suggests otherwise I would be pleased to see it. So, no doubt, would many other people who share these perceptions.

I make these observations not to undermine our Profession or our industry, because I don't believe it was uniquely in the gift of either to deliver much else (though I do lament our lack of public discourse on a number of the underlying issues, a subject I consider further in the next section). On the contrary I believe the underlying causes are largely *systemic,* and that some extend well beyond the confines of the Financial Services industry.

I cannot help thinking, however, that if our Profession invested as much effort in serving the public interest as it does in serving the interests of its members and its employers, the public might be in possession of rather more insightful information about what's really going on inside UK Financial Services plc.

7.   Actuaries and the Public Interest

As will be apparent from earlier references to the subject, I do not believe that anyone who uses the yardstick of the Profession's public interest obligations as their guide could conclude that the Profession has distinguished itself in recent years.

Curiously for a Profession that not only understands the value of experience analysis but relies on it to support so much of its work, little time thus far seems to have been devoted to a review of the Profession's own recent experience as a means of gauging how effective it has been in fulfilling its public interest role.

Three possible explanations present themselves for this: perhaps the Profession simply does not consider it to be a subject of enough importance to warrant reflection; perhaps it doesn't wish to do so for fear of what it might find; or perhaps, in much the same way as many a good counsellor can sometimes struggle with the task of keeping their own emotional house in order, the Profession finds difficulty in applying its peerless analytical skills to certain aspects of its own history.

If the first, I disagree; if the second, I think the Profession needs a better reason not to look; if the third, I would like to help. For whatever the reason, it appears to me that the Profession is missing an opportunity to learn.

With that objective in mind, I now turn to exploring the public interest question in more detail.

In principle, if 'public' is defined narrowly to be the customers of the organisations that we serve, then at an individual level, and in respect of the roles that we undertake for those organisations, I would support the view that *in general* we do a pretty good job in protecting the public interest. Indeed it has been one of the strong traditions of our Profession to do so.

But in practice the public interest extends far wider than this, and there ought to be more to our public interest role than this. Yet when it comes to matters of public interest that transcend the specific responsibilities of its individual members, the Profession often seems to have very little to say.

The Sound of Silence

Why is the Profession's discourse on any of the more substantive matters of public interest so limited?

A number of possible explanations present themselves:

1) A lack of clarity as to exactly what the Profession's public interest responsibilities actually are;

2) The absence of an effective mechanism for ensuring that matters of public interest are raised and represented;

3) The difficulty of reaching agreement or consensus as to what an appropriate line of public discourse should be (a kind of merger-style 'analysis paralysis');

4) Complacency, leading the Profession to place too much reliance on the efficacy of its individual members in supporting matters of public interest as part of their individual roles, and leaving discourse on issues of wider public interest to others (Government, the regulator or the ABI for example);

5) A conflict of interest. That commercial and public interest are not always aligned is nothing new, but the gap between the two has grown in recent years. Perhaps the Profession's desire to maintain proximity to the first is increasingly undermining its effectiveness in serving the second;

6) In the wake of the Morris Review, the strategic focus of the Profession's activity has shifted towards providing support for individual members and away from ensuring that the Profession's collective responsibilities are represented effectively, resulting in correspondingly less focus on matters of wider public interest.

On the measure of its words, exactly where the boundaries of the Profession's public interest responsibilities lie is a matter open to some interpretation.

On the measure of its deeds, however, the Profession's actual contribution to public discourse in recent years suggests that in practice it is drawing the boundaries of that responsibility as narrowly as possible.

Whatever the reasons for our collective reticence, I think it is important that we find a cure. In challenging times such as these maintaining a diplomatic silence is rather more damaging to our reputation, in part because it leaves those so-minded – of which there are a growing number – to conclude that we are paying lip service to our public interest responsibilities, in part because threats to the wider public interest have never looked greater, and in part – as we have regrettably had cause to witness too frequently in recent years - because a news agenda not informed by our Profession's collective moral lead will instead find sustenance in its individual moral failings.

Perhaps, then, it is time that the Profession's public interest credentials were subjected to a little more scrutiny.

An Analysis of Experience

Paragraph 2.3 of the Profession's own Conduct Standards has this to say about out the nature of its public interest responsibilities:

"The Actuarial Profession has an obligation to serve the public interest. Collectively it seeks to do so by informed contribution to debate on matters of public interest and by influencing those with power to protect and enhance the public interest"

A review of the profession's website or the speeches of various Faculty and Institute Presidents over the years provides further substance to the importance that our Profession purports to attach to this element of its role.

Our website puts it thus: *"The Profession is passionate about identifying matters of public concern where our input and involvement can be of benefit to society"*.

Fine words. But to what extent has the Profession lived up to them? Or for that matter, to what extent does the public believe that we have lived up to them?

In the spirit of good customer service, if the Profession wished to gain a better understanding of perceptions about that, perhaps a survey of wider opinion might be worthwhile.

In truth, however, I doubt this would tell us anything that the application of cold logic could not pre-empt. When I reflect on the above description of the Profession's public interest responsibilities in light of events and the totality of its discourse in recent years I am left thinking that it borders on the duplicitous. Only at an individual level, and to the extent demanded by regulation and our individual employers, would I conclude that the Profession has been at all effective in dispensing that responsibility.

Although the Profession's website does devote one of its pages to elaborating on the means by which the Profession aims to give substance to its public interest strapline, when it comes to the question of specifically what constitutes a matter of public interest very little is explicitly ruled in, and very little is explicitly ruled out.

Returning to first principles and applying the most basic of analysis techniques to the subject, three rather simple questions spring to mind:

1) Who are our public?
2) Which of their many interests are we seeking to represent?
3) How do we propose to represent them?

Beyond making the observation that the Profession presently seems to place too much emphasis on the individual and too little emphasis on the collective, I don't seek to explore 3) further at this stage, as the question can only properly be answered when 1) and 2) are clearly understood.

In relation to 1), several possibilities present themselves.

If one views defence of the public interest to be a commitment of the Profession as a whole to serve the public as a whole, then 'public' could be taken to mean all UK citizens. If, however, the Profession's public interest responsibilities are viewed as being expedited by its individual members through the companies that they serve, in this age of increasing globalisation such geographical boundaries lose their validity. In extremis, such thinking would lead us to a definition of 'public' that extended to the World's population – not a particularly practical interpretation!

A definition more focused on our sphere of influence might restrict it to *only* those people who are customers of the companies or organisations that we serve. Such a definition would fit well with one of our core responsibilities as individual actuaries, namely to protect the interests of the customers and members of the institutions we advise.

More esoterically one might reasonably ask whether there is any generational dependency in our definition of 'public'. In a World whose economic system exhibited long term stability that question might be academic, but in today's world of growing inter-generational debt it is anything but.

Which of these views of 'public' does our Profession subscribe to? I find it a little embarrassing to admit it, but I for one do not know.

So much for 'public'. What, then, of 'interest'?

We could opt for a narrow definition of 'interest' restricted to the financial performance of the specific products and services upon which as individuals we offer advice. Or we could expand this to embrace financial matters outside our immediate sphere of influence, but which nevertheless have impact upon our areas of Professional responsibility. In its widest sense we could interpret 'interest' to mean anything that has a significant effect on the finances of the nation, or its post-globalisation equivalent of anything that has a potentially significant impact on the World economy.

Guidance on our own website on the subject lists 'contributing to the debate on Government policy in financial matters' as one of our public interest objectives, which could be viewed as pitching our interests somewhere between the second and third of these options – but such further guidance as is offered is far from clear.

Whatever interpretation one thinks is reasonable, I don't think the present degree of ambiguity is helpful. It is not for me to put flesh on the bones of our Profession's public interest principles, but I do think that so central a component of what we stand for warrants more than a skeleton. As a Profession we should have a clearer collective understanding of what form that responsibility should take, particularly given the profile that matters of public interest are now attracting.

This increasing focus, and the increasing gravity of public interest concerns in general, reinforces the need for our Profession to be clear about where the boundaries of its public interest responsibilities actually lie. That clarity is needed to properly manage the expectations of those who rely on our services, and it is needed so that each of us as individual members of the Profession has a clear enough understanding of the underlying principles to be able to properly support the Profession in its quest to apply them in practice.

Even if one assumes that the present degree of ambiguity is intentional and that the Profession wishes to preserve flexibility in its definition for good reason, there is surely still some value in the Profession reflecting on its own experience, with particular regard to whether, and to what extent, it considers it has met its public interest obligations in relation to some of the events that have shaped the recent history of both the Profession and the industry in which it operates.

With this in mind I have included a simple public interest questionnaire as an Appendix to this paper. It includes a selection of provocative questions relating to various industry topics that may or may not be considered to fall within scope of our Profession's public interest mandate as presently defined. Some of these are quite specific and some more general, and some relate to recent history while some are more pertinent to the challenges of today.

I originally included them in the hope that they might serve as a practical tool to help the Profession reflect on its public interest contribution, give more substance to its public interest mandate and provide a greater degree of clarity to both its membership and to the public about what the Profession actually considers its public interest obligations to be.

However, the experience of bringing this paper 'to market' has led me to curtail my expectations. Given the Profession's lack of enthusiasm to promote the agenda of the paper as a whole, there seems little reason to suppose that it will show any greater willingness to engage in a debate about one of its principal subjects of contention.

Nevertheless I still hope that some readers might find time to reflect on the questions posed if only to test the boundaries of their own thinking on a subject that is, on paper at least, so central to the Profession's values and purpose.

Continuing Professional Development and the Public Interest

If the Profession is genuinely passionate about serving the public interest, should it not consider placing a mandatory public interest requirement on each of its members? As I seek to explore later in these pages, there is no shortage of causes to which an investment of time and effort could usefully be devoted.

The irony of the present mandatory CPD system is that the kind of problems that led to its introduction are fundamentally not addressed by it. As such it is a poor answer to the very pertinent question of how the Profession ensures that its members fulfil their public interest obligations.

The root of most of the problems that the Profession has latterly faced, and continues to face, lies not in a lack of core skills, technical training or understanding, but in the human frailties that on occasion lead to failure of the daily tripartite balancing act each of us is required to maintain between the pursuit of self-interest, corporate interest and the public interest. That failure happens because some of us have a predisposition on occasion to compromise the latter in pursuit of the first two. There is no magic cure for that, and no amount of CPD can eradicate it, but an obligation to invest more time in support of the public interest would at least help to restore some balance to the susceptible mindset.

The big public interest questions tend to fall outside the boundaries of what one might loosely term 'corporate responsibility' (ensuring policyholder's reasonable expectations are met, ensuring regulatory requirements are met and ensuring that the companies we serve remain solvent). Yet few of us invest much if any of our professional time servicing them. Moreover the same bias towards corporate interest is evident in many of our CPD initiatives, not least because corporate interests indirectly or directly fund many of the events.

In that sense mandatory CPD could even be seen as more of a hindrance than a help. If one accepts that it is good for actuaries to spend more time thinking outside the corporate box about matters of public interest, and that in general they are most likely to do so when not explicitly on company duty, then the time available for most people to devote to it is usually squeezed somewhere between the demands of a high-pressure job, the needs of family and the want of a social life – the same slot that mandatory CPD competes for.

If, on the other hand, every actuary was required to invest a proportion of their time each year in support of public interest initiatives that sit *demonstrably outside* their normal corporate responsibilities, this would give much-needed impetus and substance to the Profession's oft-quoted public interest mandate in this area. Such a step could also help create a market in actuarial services outside the traditional business areas, thereby facilitating the Profession's transition from old World to new through a progressive policy initiative before the next big financial storm hits us, rather than through the usual mechanism of picking up the pieces afterwards. The list of possible interest areas I explore in the last section of this paper offers ample opportunity for such 'public interest' R&D, and I am sure there are plenty more.

The Future

Where does the Profession's defence of the public interest go from here?

Well, there is nothing like a good crisis for focusing the mind. The scale and causes of the present bust has brought matters of public interest relating to the conduct of the Financial Services sector to the fore, and it seems reasonable to assume that this is a subject that will continue to attract more attention and debate in future than it has on occasion in the past.

Given this changing climate, I. would advance the following arguments in support of a big increase in the Profession's investment in this area:

1) It will be damaging to the Profession's reputation for its public interest deeds to continue to fall short of its public interest obligations;

2) The Profession has virtually no presence in the public consciousness, and this would be a positive and effective way for it to build one;
3) The investment would offer a far better return on intellectual capital than some of the present activities that occupy our Professional time;
4) It would help bring better balance to the pursuit of the Profession's tripartite interests (members, corporate, public) in a way that mandatory CPD does not;
5) The alternative is that we continue to leave matters of long term public interest for others to pursue. In which respect, look at our present generation of political leaders and consider whether you believe your grandchildrens' future to be in safe hands.

I consider this last point to be particularly pertinent, and I return to explore it in more detail in section 10.

If the Profession is to make any progress in this area, clearly it is going to need first to find its public interest voice. And while a good first step down the road would be to have greater clarity and a common understanding of what the Profession's public interest responsibility looks like in practice, as I've made reference to elsewhere in this paper I believe there are a number of other obstacles that the Profession must overcome.

Key among them is the difficulty the Profession appears to have in bringing any debate about change to a timely and successful conclusion (witness the protracted merger discussions) and a strategy that is too introspective in its focus.

A radical rethink is required, and an honest and open debate of the relevant principles would be a good place to start. One thing, however, should already be abundantly clear: leaving matters of wider long term public interest to be pursued and represented by the individual has not been effective, for the simple reason that it does not work.

8.   The Trials of Corporate Life

Symptoms of Dysfunction

Among the many polls that MORI conduct each year is the 'Trust in Professions' survey, the most recent of which was carried out in September 2009.

Few will have been surprised to see politicians languishing yet again in last place, with just 13% of adults polled believing that they can be trusted to tell the truth. But what does it say about the health of our companies that in the same survey only 25% of those polled believe that our present generation of business leaders can be trusted to tell the truth?

While that percentage might be enough to stifle progress in an Institute of Actuaries vote, it hardly amounts to a ringing endorsement of corporate well-being. And while it is true that asking the question in the wake of the banking crisis and in the midst of recession is not the best timing to elicit a positive response, the result in the previous years' survey (30%) was not appreciably better.

It is worth reflecting for a moment on what these results are telling us. That ordinary people cannot relate to politicians is nothing new, for the divide between 'we' and 'they' has been visibly growing for years. But in business the boundaries between 'we' and 'they' are rather less clear. Indeed 'we' and 'they' are in theory much the same people, as so many of 'us' are employed by 'them'.

To be clear, the survey was of a random selection of adults and the question related to a generic business leader, not one they might indirectly or directly work for. But let us not fool ourselves: if 75% of the adult population does not trust business leaders to tell the truth, we can safely assume that a significant fraction of those on company payrolls do not trust their own senior managers to tell the truth either.

It is a statistic that torpedoes the vision of our companies as well-run ships with harmonious and dedicated crews serving a common purpose. And while the survey did not ask which particular industry sector had most influenced the respondent's thinking, no great insight is required to gauge what the answer might be.

Neither is it difficult to find reasons for the degree of mistrust. Prior to the seminal events of 2008 it was still possible to believe that the Financial Services sector was in general functioning fairly well. Cosmetically, at least, that appeared to be the case. In truth, however, the symptoms of malaise have long been visible for anyone who cared to take a closer look. As a number of those symptoms form the substance of the public interest questions posed in the Appendix, I offer just one example here, one that happens to be quite close to home.

My father was recently advised that the interest rate on the savings account he'd held with his bank for some twenty years was being reduced to less than half the current base rate. Given that the base rate itself had just been reduced to historically low levels, you might guess that this amounted to not a lot.

It was a reduction that seemed even less defensible given how the gap between base rate and rates typically charged to borrowers had widened in the aftermath of the credit crisis, so I went to his local branch and enquired what rate of interest they would offer me as a new investor with my father's level of savings. The answer, you may not be surprised to know, was rather more. Ten times more, in fact.

Upon complaining to the bank on my father's behalf, I received a rely from the Retail Director suggesting that all my father needed to do was pop along to his local branch or call one of the banks customer service advisers. They would then talk him through what account might be better suited to his needs, and he could switch. Around 30,000 of the banks customers had already been through the process and switched to better accounts, he proudly proclaimed.

This, I was being led to believe, is what good customer service looks like. That my father was 86 years old and not in the best of health was not considered relevant. That my father - and no doubt many like him – was only really interested in how to access his savings and what rate of interest they would attract did not seem to have featured in his bank's thinking. Neither, it seems, had the obvious question of why continuing to be paid a vaguely competitive interest rate on his account should require him to keep contacting his bank whenever there is an interest rate change.

The mode of thinking betrayed by this response isn't confined to Retail Directors, and it isn't confined to banks. Insurance used to be simpler too. The practice at the root of my father's poor treatment, namely using existing customers to subsidise the offering of better terms to new customers, is a practice that will be familiar to many of you. It is the kind of practice that was leading people to disrespect our industry long before the first bank bailout.

In a wider sense, to take a helicopter view of today's Financial Services industry is to oversee a complex city, some of whose buildings reflect more the peccadilloes of their architects than the practicalities of their use, and some of whose streets seem not to have been built with public transport in mind. As often as not new has not replaced old but ended up being bolted onto it, in a process that successive Governments, with their perpetual penchant for fiddling with the building regulations and perpetual lack of appetite for modernisation, have done much to promulgate.

As the example of my father's bank account shows, this has created a culture that not only accommodates inefficiency but in some respects actively encourages it. The result has been an industry that has expanded way beyond the boundaries of its core function, and one that appears increasingly opaque to many of those it was created to serve.

In this complex financial landscape, those of us who look out from the windows of a better-regulated insurance industry on the present travails of our banking neighbours could be forgiven for feeling a little complacent. However, one does not need a particularly good memory to recall that present regulation of the insurance sector was built on the back of past failures, just as it now will be for the banking sector.

Robert Peston, in his topical book 'Who Runs Britain' [8] gives a compelling account of Britain's recent financial history in a form that has made the subject accessible to many a layperson. Peston, the BBC's well-connected business editor and a former Financial Editor of the FT, gives a substantive analysis of what has been happening in the economy in general and in the Financial Services sector in particular over the last dozen years or so.

It makes for grim populist reading, and provides plenty of evidence to substantiate the view that many of those whose interests we represent are being short-changed by today's financial system and the industry that supports it.

The Financial Services industry, in theory, is principally in the business of protecting people from financial risk and bringing benefit to people through long term financial investment. As actuaries employed across the insurance, pensions and investment fields, we support these aims in a range of different capacities.

In my view, only in the field of insurance protection can we claim to have been largely successful in fulfilling that purpose. In the other areas that we serve, big financial risks have been missed, products have been mis-sold, investment and pension funds have often been poorly managed by institutional investors, and public discourse on matters of significant financial interest to the consumer has been minimal until adverse consequence has rendered it unavoidable.

Moreover, one notable general trend that Peston's book does not mention is the systematic transfer of risk from financial institutions to their customers that has occurred over the last twenty years or so. This has taken a number of different forms, for example the move away from final salary schemes to money purchase arrangements in the pensions industry, the move towards reviewable protection policies and unitised investment products in the life and health industry, and through an increase in rating factors and expanded use of no-claim discounts in rating some PMI and general insurance products.

I don't question that some of these changes were needed, or that some of them were beneficial to many people. There is a strong argument that the realities of our modern economy, changing demographics and the impact of increasingly volatile and unpredictable financial markets rendered them inevitable. But in each instance commercial interests ensured that there was limited public discourse on the potential detrimental impact to consumers, and the changes were in general positioned as largely beneficial when in truth, as is nearly always the case when anything changes, there were plenty of losers as well as winners.

The reason for this seems clear enough. Bad news doesn't sell, and it is one of the cultural tenets of our industry that its products must be sold because they are seldom simply bought.

Unfortunately, however, some of those selling practices brought problems of their own. Bad publicity and scandal ensued, and our industry as a result found itself saddled with the cost and administrative burden of increasingly onerous regulatory requirements and several expensive clean-up operations.

There can be little doubt that our Professional reputation has to some degree suffered as a consequence of the impact this has had on the perceptions of our industry, and there can be little doubt that those perceptions have worsened in the wake of the current financial crisis. It may be a soft point to note, but the esteem in which the Financial Services industry is held can hardly ever have been lower. While there is no reason to suppose that the greedy and unscrupulous are any more prevalent in the Financial Services industry than they are anywhere else, and notwithstanding inconsistencies in the various expressions of our society's moral outrage, the important point is that in the minds of the public it is the Financial Services industry that is their favoured home, and it is through the Financial Services industry that their activities are seen to have extracted by far the greatest price.

I would find it hard to disagree. The prevailing wind of commercial interest has been blowing so strong and for so long through the industry that it seems to have left many of those responsible for leading it with something of a stoop. While that might be useful for avoiding the glare of those who now ask searching questions – not to say avoiding the industry debris that has recently landed at their feet - it is hardly the best perspective from which to gain a clear view of how the industry can better serve the public in future.

While bankers have understandably borne the brunt of the fallout thus far, and while as actuaries we might with some justification see some distance between ourselves and the rest of the banking fraternity, clearly that does not mean we are immune from its effects. High-profile stories about bankers who happen to be actuaries do not help our cause, and neither does it help that one of the few things that most people do know about actuaries (when they know anything at all) is that actuaries are well-paid financial experts, an observation to which they might readily add in present circumstances 'who failed to foresee the financial crisis'.

Given the scale of the financial fallout, it is not surprising that many voices outside the industry have been calling for financial market reform, tighter regulation, stronger governance and constraints on pay packages. Equally unsurprisingly, voices inside the industry have in general been rather more muted, beyond the usual suspects issuing the usual warnings about the dangers of interfering with market process in any way, shape or form.

Yet among the many losers in this crisis, there is one group that has been all but overlooked.

Just as whole countries can find themselves judged by the errant actions of a few political leaders, so a whole industry can find itself judged by the errant words or deeds of a handful who lead it. Thus do so many who have invested years of their working lives in good faith to promote good practice in our industry now find their efforts undermined by the misdeeds of a greedy and powerful minority who failed in their duty of governance.

Unfortunately for the vast majority of people employed by the Financial Services industry, a good proportion of those who end up leading it tend not to be of their ilk. Greed, hubris, and a preoccupation with big bonuses and short term profit do not define our industry, but in the eyes of a resentful public they appear to. Because the public defines our industry by the people who speak out on its behalf, and the people who speak out are the ones who have the most to fear should calls for reform be heeded – people who often *are* driven by greed, *are* full of hubris and *are* preoccupied with short term profit and the size of their next bonus.

Many of us understand what most of the public also intuitively knows, that these people are poor ambassadors for our industry and poor proponents of the Greater Good. It is time that their hubris was challenged, not just because it is delivering poor value to society but for the rather more selfish reason that it so unfairly labels the silent majority who simply endeavour to fulfil the demands of their job to the best of their ability.

Appropriately enough, the most notable voice of authority in support of the reform agenda thus far has come not from Government but from the FSA, with Lord Turner recently proffering the view that much of the short-term trading activity that characterises today's industry is 'socially useless' and calling among other things for the introduction of a Tobin tax on a wide range of speculative financial transaction. Government, for its part, after initially dismissing the proposals has subsequently made a politically expedient volte face – perhaps having realised that it badly needs the cash - and is not only now supportive but seems to be claiming the idea as its own. But for such a tax to be successful it would need to be levied globally, and in that respect there are still plenty of barriers to progress.

To date, beyond a banal, generic call for governance to be improved, our own Profession has added few words of its own to the debate. In the circumstances this looks like something of a missed opportunity, and reinforces the perception that the Actuarial Profession is either too conflicted or too conservative to contribute to contentious discussion. Thus is another positive PR opportunity in the process of being missed.

Life on the Inside

When as actuarial trainees we first emerge from the rigours of our formal education, little prepares us for the culture shock that is the experience of entering the world of corporate life.

That most of us start out having to juggle those responsibilities with the joys of studying for actuarial exams doesn't make the transition any easier, but at least in those early years most of us are protected from some of the more draining aspects of being on the company payroll. For as many of us later discover, the further up the career ladder we climb the greater the burden of pressure our employers can bring to bear upon us.

One of the more notable things that struck me from my own experiences of corporate life was the general difference in career dynamic I witnessed between those who drive corporate visions, missions, strategies and business plans (ie the members of a company's senior management and Executive Boards) and those whose task it is to implement and deliver them (ie the bulk of a company's employees).

Almost by definition, Board Directors and senior managers *tend* to be ambitious, *tend* to be quite ruthless in pursuit of their own personal goals, *tend* to have had fast track careers, *tend* not to have stayed too long in previous roles - or even with previous employers - and *tend* to be looking for a new challenge every few years (in which respect I once witnessed the entire Executive Board of one company I worked for change in 18 months).

Most people, of course, for a variety of reasons experience a rather different career dynamic – and it is as well for the generally health of our companies that they do, because businesses needs people who understand their nuts and bolts, particularly businesses as complex as those that comprise today's Financial Services industry. If everyone moved on as frequently as Board members typically do, the overall loss of knowledge and experience would be a crippling drain on many companies' knowledge base. Service history counts: someone needs to be familiar with the peculiarities of how things work, the product nuances, the systems issues, the bells and the whistles. And someone needs to know where the gremlins are hiding.

If there is a big people lesson from the banking crisis (beyond the obvious one of not incentivising them to do the wrong things), it is perhaps the need for those who drive a business strategically to better understand the risks posed by ineffective dialogue with those who understand it operationally. The banking crisis had many causes, but a failure on the part of everyone involved to understand what was happening was *not* one of them. Bad management and poor communication simply stopped that knowledge from being heard by those who should have been listening or being acted upon by those with executive authority.

Executive Boards need to ensure they identify the people who *really* understand the true nature of the products and services their company offers, particularly with regard to the critical functional components and the risks that they pose, and they need to *listen* to them. If they do not, then unless and until the Financial Services industry has retrenched to something more closely aligned to its original purpose and some of the many layers of complexity that characterise the industry of today have been stripped away, bad management and poor communication will continue to risk fomenting company failures and financial crises.

Their task can be compounded by other problems. While the victims of bullying at school can turn to teachers and parents for protection, for those bullied in the workplace it is not always so easy to know where to turn. Indeed some conclude that it is in their best interests to tolerate the situation rather than risk losing their job. A recent study [9] by Nathanael Fast and Serena Chen of USC in Los Angeles revealed a link between self-perceived incompetence and aggression in the workplace. Their research found that bosses who are 'in over their heads', i.e. who feel inadequately equipped to expedite their responsibilities, have a greater propensity to turn into office bullies than their peers. Such individuals, far from seeking the input of potentially better-informed members of their team, will instead often seek to undermine them.

Alongside this risk, the dichotomy of career experience between the minority who lead our financial institutions and the majority who keep them functioning creates an inherent tension that sits at the heart of many companies. It is a tension that the continual pressure to deliver short term profit and growth targets acts to exacerbate, and one that has turned many of our businesses into rather dysfunctional places to work.

While senior management thrives on a diet of change and fresh opportunities in the quest for growth, the workforce are left to manage the consequences and deliver the strategic vision while keeping the business engines running.

Targets once set must be met because bonuses depend on it. If that means whipping the business until it bleeds a little, so be it; and if market size, market share, policy sizes or profit margins cannot be increased, costs shall be cut. It is a culture that tends to leave few people occupying the healthy middle ground between disaffection and tribal loyalty (a place where we as actuaries should be, but may not always find ourselves).

Compounding the challenge, past industry failings and the pursuant tightening of regulatory and governance obligations, together with the continuing preoccupation with profit growth and a Boardroom desire to manage shareholders and analysts' expectations by bringing internal corporate order to external market chaos, have led to an explosion in internal audit, analysis and reporting requirements. It has also led to an obsession with process, as a means of demonstrating good governance, following best practice and reducing the risk of rogue activities that might lead to significant financial loss, insolvency or - worse - corporate failure on the kind of scale that delivered the banking crisis.

This has had a number of consequences. One of the most notable from an actuarial perspective is that an increasing number of trained Professionals are now finding themselves spending an increasing proportion of their time micro-managing margins, micro-managing the analysis and reporting of results and servicing standard-format risk and governance reports. For many, this trend has been accompanied by a reduction in the extent to which they are able to use their own insight, judgement and discretion as determinants of how best to invest their Professional time.

In a wider context, the focus on process has reduced the autonomy of large sections of the industry workforce. Rule-based decisions have replaced individual judgement; call centres deal with customers frustrated by recorded messages and option overload; customer service requests are met with automaton responses or escalated; process flows are managed; performance stats are endlessly collected and monitored; changes aren't made with autonomy they are logged and prioritised by committee, and everything seems to have become a system or a data problem.

Such changes have been an understandable response to industry developments. Indeed, one could advance a strong case that the interests of better governance demanded them. Yet it is clear from the present crisis, on a grand scale, that these changes have not eliminated the excesses of bad management and they do not always protect consumers from its effects.

Neither has the trend been without adverse consequence inside our businesses. The expansion in governance requirements, the emphasis on process and the associated growth in the number of audit, governance and risk management committees has left many of our financial institutions with quite rigid business infrastructures that are neither particularly efficient nor particularly adaptable to change. Moreover the reduction in autonomy of the individual is leaving many of the people employed by our industry increasingly disenfranchised from the businesses that employ them.

Traditionally, as trained Professionals with specialist skills actuaries have fared relatively well in the autonomy stakes. But as many actuaries who have worked in a financial reporting team for any appreciable time will attest to, while advances in the sophistication of the tools available have expanded their productivity, the explosion in governance, audit and reporting requirements that has accompanied this means that it has not necessarily made their working lives any easier and it has not necessarily left them feeling more satisfied in their roles.

It is not without irony that it was autonomy and creativity around Boardroom tables that delivered most of the financial scandals that led to the present level of industry regulation and supervisory control, while the consequence of that increase in regulation and control has been largely to constrain the degree of autonomy and creativity that can be exercised in the rest of the business.

These trends pose a threat to the dynamic of financial institutions and to the well-being and commitment of many of those who work for them. There are clearly no quick fixes, but the move towards a business model that is more interested in long term sustainability than it is in short term profit, and a retrenchment in focus of the Financial Services industry as a whole towards products that meet the needs of society and away from products that tickle the fancy of finance specialists and speculators, would each represent big steps in the right direction.

Life on the Outside

For those who believe the above constitutes an unduly harsh analysis of life inside our financial institutions in comparison with some of the alternatives, I offer this in the interests of providing a more balanced view.

I left the consultancy practice where I began my career in 1991, after six years service. One of the reasons I left was because I felt the company had become too driven in its quest for financial growth and not driven enough in its quest for much else.

Like all companies they were in business to make money, though in this case they were making it for themselves rather than feeding it to shareholders. If you could afford the fees they would advise, from behind the odd Chinese wall on occasion if need be. The gulf between charge out rates and salaries ensured nobody was under any illusion about the benefits of partnership, and the company made clear the route by which it expected people to get there.

For some colleagues chargeable time had the semblance of being an outlet for their testosterone, for others the motivation was purely financial. For all there was the incentive of a monthly league table to avoid propping up. Rumour had it that one chap once charged more than twenty four hours in one day, a feat he allegedly achieved by working while his airline chased daylight across the international date line. Whether it was true or not didn't really matter. The point is that it was believable.

No criticism of my employer is intended. I am sure that they were not doing anything that other consultancies weren't doing at the time, or haven't been doing since. I mention this only to dispel the notion, should it need dispelling, that actuarial consultancies tend to be any more predisposed to the pursuit of long term public interest over short term profit than many of their clients are.

The Business Planning Cycle

If a project goes spectacularly wrong, its failings can nearly always be traced back to events in the planning stage.

Think of The Dome, Wembley Stadium, the Olympic Village, the London Underground, the Scottish Parliament and projects to deliver new IT systems to DVLA and the NHS, among others.

Depending on your point of view, you may see these as shining examples of Government incompetence, as shining examples of civil service inefficiency, or as an illustration of the degree to which the private sector will happily fleece taxpayers when provided with an opportunity. You may even see them as a combination of the three. But what few people would dispute is that all could have benefited from better planning.

Conventional wisdom has it that the private sector is rather more efficient in its planning, though given that the average budget overspend on Government-sponsored projects in the last few years has been over 30% [10], and given how late a number of high-profile public sector projects have been delivered, one might argue that it would be a concern if they were not.

But the truth is that bad planning is far from confined to the public sector. A lack of clear definition at the requirements stage, often in combination with a lack of clearly defined accountabilities, has been a feature of any number of Board-sponsored projects I have witnessed over the years.

On a grander, more visible scale, if one is charitable and presumes that the motivation of high street banks here and in America wasn't to embark on the World's biggest Ponzi scheme, what kind of planning process allowed Northern Rock, HBOS, RBS and any number of other financial institutions to take the risks that they did with the consequences that we have witnessed?

Anyone seeking to reassure themselves that this is largely a banking problem will not find it in the plight of AIG, and anyone who has been closely involved in the business planning cycle of their own company may well have witnessed at close quarters some of the reasons why very bad decisions are sometimes made by very large companies, even those that aren't banks.

Conceptually at least, the business planning cycle has much to commend it. Every year the company reappraises its performance against strategic objectives in the context of its risk appetite, reviews progress against deliverables of all major projects, analyses its financial results, examines the market, has an inclusive discussion about development imperatives and priorities, updates its strategic plan objectives and financial targets accordingly and translates the resulting plan into a cascaded series of objectives that people at all levels of the business can both understand and contribute to delivering.

If this was how it worked in all our major institutions I venture to suggest that the present financial crisis would have been rather less severe in its impact – maybe even averted - and our financial system might at least be a little better placed to ride out some of the storms that lie ahead.

Unfortunately, in many cases this is not how it works in practice. Indeed it hasn't worked that way in any financial institution whose planning process I have yet witnessed (six, and counting).

The simple truth is that while the business planning process yearns for inclusivity, business demands always seem to contrive to ensure that it never quite finds the time for it. Instead the process typically manifests the tension I referred to earlier. In the confluence of top-down and bottom-up views, however, the scales are tipped firmly in the favour of the former. Shareholders have expectations, bonuses depend on them, and if they are not met it could cost a CEO his job, his reputation or both. Power sits in the hands of those who set strategy, not those who are tasked with delivering it.

Conventional wisdom, as espoused by many an Executive Board member, is that a bottom-up planning process places too much emphasis on present reality and not enough emphasis on future potential, will as a result tend to see more obstacles than opportunities and thereby tend to deliver targets that are not sufficiently stretching. Companies need strategic thinkers, and conventional wisdom says that the best strategic thinkers are those who've thought strategically for lots of companies, not spent their working lives dealing with the challenges and problems of only one.

Notwithstanding the evident convenience of this argument for those it serves, it undoubtedly does have some merit. However, the equivalent limitations in top-down thinking are less frequently acknowledged. Executive Boards are employed to drive change and paid to deliver growth. Our financial system is not programmed to expect anything less. And if that requires squeezing the business by cutting costs or headcount so be it. There is only one financial tune, and all must dance to it.

Thus do considerations of present reality sometimes find themselves crushed under the weight of future expectation, and thus do some Boards find themselves taking decisions that run counter to the long term interests of their businesses and taking excessive risks in the pursuit of profit.

For our financial system ensures that people tend to be appointed to Executive Boards not for what they know but what it is believed they can deliver, and while Executive Boards may be presumed to know what is best for their businesses they are paid to deliver short term profit.

As we have now seen to our substantial collective cost, this model doesn't always deliver Executive Boards who act in the long term interests of anyone - including, on occasion, even themselves.

In essence, then, the limitations of the present approach to business planning can be characterised thus: a financial system whose focus is the delivery of short term returns; a reward system whose focus is incentivising delivery of this; a management culture of perpetual change that leaves many Executive Board members disconnected from and often having insufficient understanding of some of the risks and issues affecting their businesses; and an overarching ethos that whatever is presently done or delivered must always be improved upon.

Under this approach it is little wonder then that the corporate planning process often fails to translate Executive Board strategy into a plan that employees can empathise with, and little wonder that instead our industry has come to rely increasingly upon financial incentives to ensure that targets are delivered.

In this environment, career progression is dictated by the need to get on with one's peers, impress one's superiors and ensure one's team delivers its objectives. We must treat customers fairly, but few people's career paths will be illuminated by devotion to that cause: being seen to be aligned with, and helping to deliver, your company's growth strategy matters more for both your career prospects and your finances, And as the experience of one or two brave souls in the banking industry has illustrated, not only can dissent hamper your progress, it might even cost you your job.

Fresh from the rigours of a formal education, with our finely tuned analytical skills, enthusiasm and desire to succeed, and as actuarial trainees with the full support of our Profession, this is the environment into which our fledgling actuarial careers are launched.

As a means of promoting the kind of boldness and spirit of enterprise that the leaders of our Profession envisage, and which the World now so desperately needs, this is like firing arrows into treacle. For enterprise in the corporate sense is a rather different animal, one that has too prejudicial a disposition to meet the longer term needs of either the Profession or the public it is mandated to serve.

How might this be changed?

Well, perhaps the first thing to note is that greater intervention and stronger regulation would have their limitations even if Government did have an appetite for them. The principle of regulation is that if you can't change the animal's behaviour then you can at least seek to contain it, but the difficulty is that containment is a lot more straightforward – not to say cost-effective - in zoos than it is in business.

It would clearly be better if the bulk of errant behaviour could be addressed without the need for greater regulation. The obvious answer is stronger and more effective corporate governance, responsibility for which sits with company Boards. In that respect, the role of non-Executive Directors in particular is crucial in ensuring and independent and objective view of matters of corporate risk and reward is maintained at all times.

To witness the extent to which both risk and reward can spiral out of control under this system of governance, however, one needs only to survey the wreckage of the present financial crisis. A more effective control mechanism is evidently required.

As in so many other areas touched upon in this paper, it is clearly neither in the gift of the Profession to impose governance solutions nor in its mandate to do so. But the Profession is going to struggle to fulfil its risk management aspirations if it continues to fail to articulate its own corporate governance vision in response to the scale of failure we have just witnessed. For while there are undoubtedly things that we can do as individuals to promote better governance (some of which I consider below) if the Profession is to exercise any effective influence over policy in this area it will need to do so with a collective voice. On key questions such as this the individual view is often not heard, and is too easy to ignore even when it is.

In the hope of breathing some life into the debate, here is one suggestion.

It seems to me that more independent scrutiny of the plans and activities of large financial institutions is required, and that this is best achieved by ensuring input from, and preferably requiring signoff by, a person or persons who meet the following requirements:

- Someone who is close enough to the business and its financial dynamic to offer an informed and enlightened view of business plan proposals
- Someone whose role includes accountability for representing the long term public interest
- Someone whose ability to act in this capacity is not compromised by financial incentives dependent on company performance

Final point at present notwithstanding, does anyone spring to mind?

In the current climate, I believe there are plenty of good reasons beyond the last bullet point above why it might be appropriate for actuaries employed by financial institutions to forego incentives linked to company financial performance - a proposition I consider in more detail in the next section.

If they were to do so, who would be better placed to play a central role within the business in ensuring business plans represented a proper balance of long term and short term interests, and of policyholder and shareholder concerns?

On occasion in the past when bearing witness to some of the more outlandish plan assumptions that are on occasion foisted upon our businesses, I've wondered what market picture would emerge if one were to take the key business plan assumptions of all the major providers and aggregate them. At the very least the end result would amount to a telling barometer of business optimism, and if I were a regulator seeking to gain comfort that companies were well-governed and acting in the long term interests of their customers I would consider their corporate plan might be a good place to start looking.

There may yet come a time when regulatory intervention extends to ensuring the collection of certain relevant basic information about corporate business plans from all major financial institutions. For all the complexities of individual businesses it would not be difficult to extract the key measures of business dynamic from each, for example assumptions about market growth, market share, the assumed level of change in sales, margin and expenses and the assumed impact of unwinding extant business.

Even without such formal intervention, there ought to be a more effective role for actuaries to play in ensuring that the business plans of some of their employers are as supportive of the long term public interest as they are of short term business priorities.

Radical, perhaps. Fraught with practical challenges, perhaps. But can we at least not recognise that there is a problem, that it isn't one that sits solely with banks, and that as a Profession we ought to be devoting more time to discussing how best it might be addressed?

Every Little Helps

Regardless of whether Government, regulators and/or the Actuarial Profession deign to play a greater role in addressing some of the root causes of poor corporate governance, there is still much that can be done at an individual level.

The reluctance of those who lead us, be they in Parliament, Industry or the Professions, to change course when confronted with changing reality gives succour to those who, for the want of an easy life, wish to wait for others to lead before changing their own behaviour, even if at some level they understand that their own complicity and inertia is contributing to the problem.

This is an attitude that is as flawed as it is prevalent. The gravity of the World's situation, and on a smaller scale that faced by our Profession, is such that the respective challenges both face could not be solved purely by strong leadership even if it were forthcoming. Just as a good business plan needs support from the top down and the bottom up to be effective, so any response to the challenges that now confront us will need to be met at the level of the strategic and the individual if it is to be effective.

'Think global, act local' is not a new catchphrase (it is documented as having been used by a Scottish town planner way back in 1915, oddly enough) but it is one that has grown much in currency in recent years, in recognition of the global nature of many of the challenges we now face and as a means of confronting the inertia that many of us (rather conveniently) feel when questioning the significance of any individual contribution we might otherwise be minded to make.

The phrase is not without significance for the UK Actuarial Profession either; 'think global' could be seen as having a clear strategy that directs the activities of the Profession as a whole and a leadership that has a clear idea of how it should best be implemented, and 'act local' could be seen as what we each ought to be doing outside the confines of our individual job responsibilities to progress that wider agenda.

As I have sought to set out in this paper, I believe the Profession's current introspective strategy to be particularly ill-equipped to help confront the big challenges we all face today and particularly ill-equipped to fulfil the Profession's grand visions of tomorrow. But while the deeds of the Profession and those of its individual members would undoubtedly be more effective if they were to act in unison, in the quest for a greater good the relative impotence of the former is no cause for abdication of responsibility on the part of the latter.

Indeed one could argue quite opposite. What is true for energy conservation is also true of actuarial endeavour: every little helps. While it might be tempting to use inertia of the Profession as a whole as an excuse for not pushing back within our own individual spheres of influence, I venture to suggest that the situation we presently find ourselves in does not really afford us that luxury.

While I claim no particular expertise as to how such influence as is within our individual gift might best be exercised, everyone's experience has some value and during the course of writing this paper I have had cause to spend some time reflecting on my own. In that respect, I feel fortunate in having had opportunities to work both inside and outside the Profession, in consultancy and in industry, and both on and off the payroll.

One of the more noteworthy features of that experience is that I have never felt particularly aligned to the vision of any company I have had the pleasure of serving - including, incidentally, my own - despite considerable investment on the part of some of them to enlighten me.

I think I came to realise at quite an early stage in my career that I was not particularly 'clubbable'. On one memorable occasion I recall having had my back massaged by a work colleague as part of a management bonding exercise, an experience that might have been slightly more enjoyable had I not at the same time been required to serve up the same treatment to someone sat in front of me. By the end of that day I was left feeling less that the company had a vision I could align myself with and more that the MD was a fruitcake. As he was dismissed shortly afterwards, perhaps I was not alone.

None of which experience particularly qualifies me to advise anyone else as to how they should approach their own working life, but it did leave me thinking that the temptation to embrace club membership doesn't always sit comfortably with the need to maintain an independent, objective view.

So for what it is worth, here is my own pick & mix of ideals I've endeavoured over the years (with varying degrees of success) to adopt in my own working life. Whether you regard them as helpful or heresy, I hope you might find them worthy of a moment's reflection:

- Don't passively subscribe to your employer's vision and values. Hold on to your own, contrast the two, and where they are at odds ask relevant questions (of your employer, or yourself!)
- Don't just think TCF and CPD, think how much of what you're doing is in the long term public interest and look for opportunities to increase it
- Don't presume that the past is a guide to the future. It may well not be
- Don't judge the value of a process, principle or paradigm by how long it has been adhered to, or by whom
- Don't let loyalty, greed, ambition or fear compromise your long term vision, or the fortitude with which you pursue it

- Don't let club membership (professional, political, business or otherwise) compromise your impartiality. Learn to recognise tribal loyalty in yourself and in others, and be aware of how it can cloud your judgement (and theirs)
- Don't presume that seniority is linked to the exercising of sound judgement
- Don't presume that professional qualification is linked to the exercising of sound judgement either
- Don't let issues or concerns fester: tackle them at source
- Don't presume that the pursuit of self-interest, corporate interest and the long term public interest are always aligned, and remember which one your Profession was founded to serve
- Be absolutely clear about your responsibilities and your objectives, and to the extent it is within your influence, ensure others are clear about theirs.
- *Always* fight to maintain an independent view
- Don't judge the worth of what you do by how much you're paid to do it

My special thanks to Fred Goodwin, ex CEO of RBS, a chartered accountant by training and with 20 years experience in the banking industry, for having single-handedly giving substance to so many of them. Mnemonics of so fitting a physical embodiment are rare, but most useful.

The last three bullets I am particularly passionate about. If one is to judge by the extent to which, when anything goes wrong, so many are able so successfully to deny responsibility for so much, carefully crafted ambiguity seems to be reaching epidemic proportions these days. This ambiguity is the enemy of accountability, allowing those who take credit when things go well to avoid culpability when things go badly. Fight this disease wherever you find it.

Reference maintaining an independent viewpoint, over the years I have lost count of the number of courses and meetings I have attended at which I've been encouraged to 'think outside the box'. On no occasion do I recall anyone being minded to give a decent description of what 'the box' actually was, but I was always under no illusion that the one box everyone was happy for my thinking not to stray beyond was a box marked 'corporate interest'.

With regard to the last bullet point, as actuaries with public interest responsibilities we ought to be better placed than most to recognise a socially useless activity when we see it. Yet most of the time most of us simply do as we are told, because we are paid by someone to do it. Professor Garciano's comments in response to the Queen's pertinent question should be ringing in our ears.

In benign times, the cost of smart people indulging in socially useless activities is a cost that our industry and society as a whole can absorb. Indeed, it did. However it is the central hypothesis of this paper that we are entering a period that, far from being benign, will be seminal to our history. It is a period in which society will need smart people to be utilising their skills to more socially-productive effect. Furthermore I believe that if we all wait for that to change from the top down (as one day, it will), by then it may well be too late. If we are indeed members of a Profession that understands risk, then we should recognise this as a risk that is not worth taking.

Nobody needs to go as far as our police force is trained to do (the ABC of policing: Assume nothing; Believe nothing; Challenge everything), but as we have seen all too clearly of late maintaining an independent perspective, questioning rather than accepting and challenging rather than acquiescing are vital to good governance. Small events can beget big consequences: who knows, while company bosses may not always welcome your intervention, your grandchildren may yet one day have cause to.

I can't help thinking that if a few more people inside the banking industry had been working to principles similar to those listed above then the scale of devastation wreaked by the present financial crisis might have been much reduced. And while better governance and regulation may already be better protecting the insurance sector from the kind of excesses that have brought banking sector to its knees, we should not fool ourselves into thinking that the underlying behaviours and motivations of some of those who presently lead it are so very different.

9. Of Governance and Government

Over the last thirty years, there have been perhaps four forces that have shaped our politics and successive governments more than any others.

The first, and most evident, has been the narrowing of ideological difference between the main parties of Government. Depending on whether one is looking to the past or the future, this is either the proponents of Capitalisms' greatest success or our two party-dominated electoral system's greatest failure.

The second is rooted in the composition of our governing elite. Once upon a time we had fewer career politicians and more people who entered politics after spells in industry or from other public service roles. This helped to produce a more integrated style of government, one where the implications of policy were challenged more insightfully and rigorously than they often are today, and one where politicians had a better understanding of the business dynamic – including, perhaps, a greater ability to recognise when they were being hoodwinked. It may also have helped to produce Governments whose representatives were less prejudiced by the lure of lucrative post-ministerial private sector appointments.

The third big change in political dynamic, driven largely by our present Government, has been the dilution in effectiveness of the traditional instruments of our democracy (Government by Cabinet, House of Commons debate and parliamentary vote) through increasing centralisation of power. By tradition MPs in general and Cabinet Ministers in particular tend to toe their party line, and in that respect it has been notable how many have broken ranks in recent years to denounce the extent to which Government by collective has been undermined. For anyone who thinks this has had a beneficial impact on the quality of post-election Government in relation to pre-election commitments, New Labour's last two manifestos make interesting reading.

The fourth big influence on the quality of Government relates to the efficacy of the instruments of state that Government traditionally relies upon for it to function. It would be interesting to witness how a FTSE 100 company would fare if it were managed in the same manner and using the same quality of information as that used to run some Government departments and much of the public sector.

The most unfortunate aspect of this, in light of the growing list of failures being clocked up by the private sector, is that public sector inefficiency has become part of the Capitalist mantra: no matter how great the failings of the free market, the alternative, we are told, will always be worse.

This notion has been with us for so long that for many it has the feel of an accepted truth, as if public service inefficiency were a chronic condition that we should not expect to respond to treatment. Successive Governments, through their own failure to treat it, have reinforced that perception. Yet while the argument that it is for Government to put its own house in order clearly has some justification, there are also wider considerations.

Firstly, Government is not always keen to take the kind of steps necessary to address public sector inefficiency. While the long term public interest would recognise that someone in an unnecessary or inefficient public sector role is in effect already on benefits, through Government eyes any public sector redundancy is bad news for the unemployment register, another drain on the welfare state and another dent in the tax take, all of which form part of the currency of short term politics.

Secondly, while our modern Capitalist system's exploitation of greed over moral conscience in the quest for profit may have many manifestations - stretching from the dumping of toxic assets through the discounting of toxic liabilities to the dumping of toxic waste - in few of them is it more explicit or pervasive than in the manner in which Government contracts are exploited by the private sector. All too often they are seen as a license to print money for the few, not an opportunity to save it for the many.

Instead, then, we have a situation where huge projects and huge chunks of the public sector with multi-million pound budgets continue to be managed badly using poor-quality information. The NHS, for example, with an annual budget that swallows around £90bn of public money, is run on a paucity of management information that would cause heads to roll if it were a quoted company. Nobody inside or outside the NHS can currently say how much of its annual budget is spent on external consultants, let alone whether it is getting a good return on the investment. That is a matter of the utmost public interest, particularly given the present parlous state of the public finances, yet still few inroads appear to have been made into the problem.

The truth about public sector waste is as ever rather less simplistic than some popular soundbites suggest. Public sector inefficiency is not the result of a paucity of talent among those it employs, any more than it is due to a lack of financial incentives for public sector workers. Rather, its origins lie largely in management failure and poor governance. In which respect it is unfortunate that so few actuaries have thus far made inroads into the sector, for it is hard to imagine a bigger test or a better cause for the deployment of the business management skills which as actuaries we often claim as complements to our core training.

Alongside the basic changes in political fabric described above, and not unrelated to them, the last two decades have witnessed a succession of scandals, mishaps and more scandals. This has taken its toll on the public's perception of the political class as a whole, with a damaging and pervasive loss of trust in people's perceptions of politicians' ability or willingness to properly represent the long term public interest.

The response thus far has been depressingly familiar. In the aftermath of the financial crisis there was much talk of the need for fundamental reform of the banking sector, but little has thus far changed. In the wake of the MPs expenses scandal there was much talk of the need to reform politics, but thus far little has changed. Public will is defied with impunity (witness disgraced ex-speaker Michael Martin's appointment to the House of

Lords). Would-be celebrity MPs step forward to make their moral point, but both we and they know that the issues run far deeper.

The price of this is now becoming increasingly apparent. For while the worst of the present financial crisis may now be behind us, global warming, peak oil and other forces I referred to in section 5 are gathering forces to sink the ideological ship that both mainstream parties are continuing to sail on our behalf. And as yet, no rescue vessel is in sight.

An over-dramatic metaphor, perhaps. But the point I labour is that we are in urgent need of an alternative vision, yet the moral authority, and perhaps the ability, of the main political parties to articulate one has been fundamentally compromised.

Looking beyond these symptoms of malaise, there is one trait above all others that those who govern us seem to share with many who make it into company boardrooms, namely the prevalence of ego. Ambition, the desire to wield power and the need to be seen as successful are all manifestations of it, and with the exception of a minority who possess public-spiritedness of saintly proportions, the prevalence of ego is surely the primary reason many modern-day politicians are prepared, on an MPs salary, to make their lives public property and risk being mauled by the tabloid press.

Unfortunately, ego doesn't always come packaged with the other traits required to ensure it is constructively channelled - intellect, a strong sense of public duty and good judgement, for example. Indeed one could (a little mischievously) suggest that the exercising of unsound judgement is a self-selecting characteristic of anyone choosing to enter Parliament these days. Much as I think our present generation of politicians are failing us, and much as I am prepared to invest the time and effort required to write what may prove to be a career-limiting paper on that and other subjects, even my own public-spiritedness would not extend to entering British politics right now.

One of the less desirable manifestations of unconstrained ego is the degree to which it is sometimes able to distort the perceptions of its host in order to protect itself. It would be less of a concern if this inability to accept culpability were confined to the odd Prime Minister, ex Speaker of the House or ex banking executive, but it is not. It pervades the higher echelons of industry and Government, and an equally pervasive lack of accountability does little to contain it.

In the last section I explored some of the people issues that can affect the efficacy of management at senior levels in both Industry and Government. Among those who lead us we have people whose egos exude confidence and ambition, who by definition will be less inclined than most to seek the counsel of others in deciding a course of action, and we have people who feel out of their depth, whose fragile egos are more predisposed to bullying subordinates than seeking help. Against this backdrop, is it any wonder that many within the rank and file of our businesses feel that their voice is not often heard?

That is not to undermine the many people in Government and around Boardroom tables who are blessed with strong intellect, sound judgement and good motive. It is just to say that there are also plenty who are not, and that in the competition to be heard the voices of the wise do not always seem to prevail. The result is what we see: among other things bad Government, banking crises and a prevalence of short-term thinking.

In a wider context, when one reflects on many of the things successive Governments have done in our name, and how far removed some of them have been from the manifestos upon which they were elected, it becomes clear just how limited a tool democratic elections alone have become as determinants of our collective future.

Once the voting is over a free press, strong media presence and good journalism go some way towards promoting greater accountability and reining in the worst excesses of bad Government, but in recent years the limitations of our present political process as an agent for promoting the Greater Good have become increasingly evident. By the time a public interest story makes headlines the deed has usually already been done; only rarely does a media campaign successfully unpick or prevent bad policy decisions. The rest of the time, with no effective control mechanism we are instead left to deal with consequence after the event. Moreover, as our next Government is already shaping up to remind us, even when we exercise our opportunity to vote the alternative can prove equally ineffective.

Corporations that have no obligations beyond those to their shareholders and customers might legitimately claim that such questions are not their concern, but a Profession with a wider public interest mandate whose members have the collective intellect, vision and skill set to make a difference cannot.

The reason I have chosen to take a closer look at Government and governance here is this: if there is one area where the past *has* proved a reliable guide to the future, it is in the inability of successive Governments to properly confront and address long term problems.

Government may yet surprise us, but until it does we should expect more of the same. And more of the same is really not what we need right now.

Government needs help, but unfortunately it does not always appear to recognise that fact. Even when it does, as often as not the advisers it appoints to help are given a flawed mandate, come neatly packaged with their own vested interests and prejudiced perspectives or meet with politicians who have their own vested interests and prejudiced perspectives.

Examples are legion. Here are a few of the more recent ones:

- The Government appointed an ex-banker to the task of implementing its policy on bank bailouts. The result was that the most notorious of failed bank Chief Executives was allowed to walk away with a pension pot of scandalous proportions, and the new Chief Executive that replaced him was recruited on a pay package of scandalous proportions, a symbolic shambles that inflicted further damage on both the industry's reputation and people's confidence in the ability of Government to properly supervise it.

- When the Government recently commissioned a report into whether and how the UK Financial Services industry needs to adapt to the challenges of tomorrow, it saw no conflict of interest in putting its authorship in the hands of senior figures from the UK Financial Services industry of today. Suffice it to say that the resulting report reads just as many people outside the industry expected it to, and did little to reassure people that the industry of tomorrow will be any more effective in serving the public need than is the industry of today.

- In similar vein, the Treasury sdaw no conflict of interest in appointing City grandee and former investment banker Sir David Walker to examine the thorny issue of bankers pay. The main conclusion of his review? Pay is best supervised through a voluntary code policed by shareholders and non-executive directors. A cynic might think that had already been tried.

- The recent appointment of Alan Sugar to the House of Lords serves perfectly to highlight wider flaws in both the Government's appointment process and in the judgement of some of those who use it. If the Government wanted to appoint someone with Sir Alan's proven abilities at hiring and firing people, they might at least have placed him in a position in which he could best utilise the skill. Nobody gets fired from the House of Lords, and given the nature of some recent appointments it seems that present entry requirements may be a little slack for Sir Alan's taste.

- The decision to appoint James Crosby to the post of Deputy Chairman of the FSA in 2004 may have appeared to some to be stretching the concept of poacher turned gamekeeper to its limit even at the time. With hindsight, it was another error of judgement that served only to reinforce public loss of confidence in the abilities of both Government and regulator to properly supervise the industry.

- Like some bankers, ministers do not always react well to being told things that they do not want to hear. This sometimes with profound consequences for the messenger and/or the public, regardless of the reputation of the adviser or the validity of their message. Thus, for example, did the Chairman of the Drugs Advisory Council recently find himself sacked for telling the truth about drugs, and thus was former UN weapons inspector David Kelly hounded to his death for being too honest in his assessment of the evidence used to justify our involvement in the Iraq war.

Little wonder, in the face of such ineptitude, that our mode of Government has been the source of so much disillusionment of late, and that so many people believe it to be increasingly ineffective.

The reality of this situation poses something of a dilemma for a public service-oriented Profession such as ours. In one respect, independent Professions are understandably reticent to engage in discourse on any subjects that may be construed to have political flavour, but in another if the body politic itself is seen on a grand scale to be failing in its duty to serve the public interest, is there not an even greater moral obligation on the Profession to do so?

Political affiliations and beliefs can distort the application of reason, as the deep-seated resistance of some in the banking industry to state intervention in the wake of the banking crisis revealed, even when the alternative was industry collapse.

But what to do when the only visions offered by the main political parties are variants of a socio-economic model that is failing badly?

The language of political right and left is long past its sell-by date. I made the point earlier that diplomatic deference to matters of right and left should not preclude comment on matters of right and wrong. Politics, economics, the public interest and matters of social justice are all inextricably linked, and in its desire to avoid all subjects it construes may relate to the first the Profession seems to be paralysing itself into near silence on the rest.

In this respect, as in others touched upon in this paper, the past should no longer be trusted as a reliable guide. To recognise the limitations of Capitalism does not make one a Communist, any more than to recognise the failures of Communism makes one a Capitalist. Fundamentally, the failings of both are rooted in the same causes: greed (for power or money), a failure to rein in the excesses that flow from it, and a failure to properly hold accountable those who promulgate them.

If we are to find a path out of our present predicament to some kind of sustainable future, it will be neither Communism nor Capitalism in their characteristic guises that get us there, and it won't be our present brand of democracy that delivers it. Instead, it will be through hard, objective analysis of the historical benefits and failings of each, a re-evaluation of priorities and the formulation of a new socio-economic model built around a far broader, less financially-oriented and more sustainable definition of wealth and prosperity, and an unwavering, long term commitment by the body politic to seek global co-operation in implementing it.

Pipe dreams don't come much bigger, do they? But I genuinely believe that it is going to take something on this scale to sort out the present mess, and I genuinely believe that the alternative is a bleak enough prospect that we should not simply through our own inaction resign ourselves to it.

Is there a role for actuaries to play in helping to drive this change? Of course there is. As an apolitical organisation with vision, analytical ability and a strong financial toolkit the Profession is very well placed to help develop a new vision. But it will not be in a position to do so without first ditching some of the dated dogma that presently constrains its thinking and stifles its voice.

The Bigger Picture

We invest billions of pounds a year in educating our children, but when it comes to educating adults about the choices we now face, our political leaders seem not just to tolerate ignorance but to actively encourage it. Is ours an information age, or the Age of Misinformation? Perhaps both.

If one presumes that people have an interest in the long term future of their offspring - and one would expect that they should – then public education is now a priority. Instead however, successive Governments, while mismanaging or misrepresenting any number of smaller risks, have continued to tiptoe fearfully around the central issue, that our present mode of existence is simply not sustainable and that something has to give. Difficult choices need to be made, but they are being deferred rather than discussed. Short term politics is subsuming long term reason, and short term expediency is parking long term problems.

What stops the Actuarial Profession from helping to bring some much-needed independent reason to the debate? Is it lack of boldness? Lack of wlll? Lack of appetite to discuss subjects that might offend commercial sensitivities? Lack of a clear policy framework? Lack of clarity as to what our public interest role is? Lack of ability to reach consensus? Lack of enthusiasm to engage on any contentious issue that can be construed as someone else's problem?

Whatever the underlying reasons, in the circumstances they amount to a poor excuse. Because from drugs policy to the terrorist threat to evidence justifying dubious wars statistics are routinely being abused and misused by those who lead us, while the risks that really ought to concern us are routinely downplayed or ignored.

If the Profession's aspirations to expand its influence in the field of risk management are to gain any credence, it had better soon find some moral backbone and start addressing the problems that have constrained it in the past. In seeking to build its risk management credentials, into what areas of risk management is the Profession seeking to expand?

Does it wish to help the cause of confronting the real risks that threaten the long term public interest, or is it to continue in its fruitless quest to manage the unmanageable, endeavouring to protect the balance sheets of those it serves from ever greater shocks? Should the Profession choose to position itself as an expert at the art of catching fallout from a failing system, it will get what it deserves. There is an urgent need for us to start tackling causes instead of simply trying to managing symptoms.

<u>A Change in Approach</u>

The Profession of today is far too timid to pass comment on the kind of public interest concerns I allude to above. As the challenges that confront us grow, so the ever-flexible boundaries of the Profession's public interest mandate seem to have shrunk to accommodate, to the point where it has little of any consequence to say about any subject that registers in the public consciousness.

With a change in mindset and approach, what benefit could we bring?

Well, anyone who has spent any appreciable time inside the Profession would never accuse it of being light on ego. However the self-selecting hurdle that our club's entry requirements represent, in the form of both academic qualification and the rigours of our Professional training, ensures that within our ranks ego does at least tend to be more frequently accompanied by two of the main agents that help to constrain its excesses, namely strong intellect and good judgement. Indeed if it isn't too egotistical of me to say so, my best guess is that our collective ego as a Profession is pitched somewhere above the population average and somewhere below that in most Boardrooms and the House of Commons, while our collective intellect and reasoning ability might *in general* tend to be somewhat higher than both.

This, together with our strong analytical skills, our understanding of statistics and ability to recognise when they are being abused or properly used, and a Professional mandate that is free from the constraints of a short term electoral cycle, in theory leaves our Profession rather better placed to offer an unbiased view on matters of long term public interest than many of those who lead us (in Government or in business).

There are challenges, of course. While intellect and sound judgement can help to protect ego from its own excess, the value of seeing a problem from many angles is undermined if the price of so doing is an inability to agree a solution. Unless he or she is happy to settle for a list of options, anyone who wanted a quick answer to a challenging problem might be best advised not to leave it with a group of actuaries to resolve.

Neither, in general, as actuaries do we have a reputation for being particularly imaginative or creative in our approach. I have some empathy with that view: such creativity as hadn't already been drummed out of me by four years spent studying mathematics at university soon found itself crushed under weight of actuarial training and analysis. It took a year spent away from the industry for me to even begin to rekindle what rather disconcertingly I barely realised I'd ever lost.

But these are minor drawbacks. The balance of attributes we do collectively possess, together with our business acumen and financial understanding, invests our Profession with huge potential, much of which I believe remains untapped. If people don't realise that they need us – and largely they don't - it is because we perpetually fail to take opportunities to demonstrate why they should. It is not for the public to change to accommodate the Profession's vision; it is for the Profession to change to better serve the public need.

On the subject of change, I do note the Profession's increased use of surveys and discussion forums of late, and it is encouraging to see these being extended to consider issues beyond the ongoing merger debate. Indeed I read with interest summary findings of the last such survey, distributed with the April edition of The Actuary.

What were its conclusions? People apparently have little or no understanding of what we do. We are too bound by our traditions, too inwardly focused, have a weak public profile and are perceived to be too detached from the people we serve.

Was this revelatory? I remember having similar thoughts back in 1991 when I first qualified.

If surveys and discussion forums are to be anything more than simply a vent for members' frustrations, they must meet with a Profession whose leadership has both a clear idea of the questions it needs to find answers to and the vision and fortitude to act accordingly. In which respect I am bound to observe, looking back on the events of recent years, vision and fortitude have been notable largely by their absence.

The incentive for doing so should be clear enough: our Profession is presently travelling down a road of diminishing returns, and our society is presently travelling down a road to its own disintegration.

While the degree of influence one Profession can exercise over wider events is clearly limited, in the circumstances that is no good reason for it not to contribute to the debate, or to provide leadership where it is lacking. There is no disgrace in failure if the cause is good, and the Profession might receive a much-needed boost for its reputation in the process, not least by demonstrating that the Profession's risk management credentials *do* have substance beyond the rhetoric, that its interests *do* extend beyond the purely commercial, and that it *does* have something constructive to say about important matters of long term public interest. And who knows, the Profession might even begin to convince the World that it really does need actuaries.

I explained earlier why I believe boldness and spirit of enterprise on the part of individual members will not be sufficient for the Profession to build (or perhaps even rebuild) its reputation and diversify its interests. The Profession *as a whole* has poor representation, for deep-seated reasons, and in the absence of a new mindset, strategy and approach I believe that the Profession is going to find expanding its influence outside its traditional areas of responsibility even more difficult in future than it has in the past. A change in mindset is needed for the Profession to unburden itself from some of the baggage of its own history, a change in strategy is needed if it is to develop a base from which to expand its influence, and a change in approach is needed if it is ever to find a voice with which to do so.

However if the Profession *can* rediscover its raison d'etre, *can* free itself from so limiting an introspective stragegy and *can* find its voice, the range of possible opportunities for it to add value, raise its profile and build its influence has never looked greater.

10. Capitalism and the Corruption of Moral Sentiments

In section 5 I sought to explore some of the limitations of economics as a science, and touched upon reasons why some of the more recent trends and developments in financial markets should be of concern to us all. In this section I seek to take a closer look at some of the characteristics of our present economic doctrine of choice and consider why these too should concern us

Given the nature and scale of the havoc that has been wreaked by the latest bust, it is perhaps not surprising that, among the usual voices that always call for change in every downturn of the economic cycle, many more are now questioning whether the economic model that allowed it to happen might itself be unfit for purpose. It is a very pertinent question.

That it is being challenged by mainstream opinion at all is significant, and the fact that, at the time of writing, beyond calls for tighter regulation and better governance, any consensus as to what shape economic reform might take hasn't yet even begun to emerge should not disguise the underlying change in sentiment. There may be little sign as yet of any fundamental change in mindset in Westminster or around Britain's Boardroom tables, but the seeds of reform are being sown in the changing mindset of an increasingly disillusioned public.

The public are growing increasingly disillusioned because they can see what most of our politicians and business leaders choose not to admit, that today's society is the product of a failing system.

Capitalism is central to that failure, and I believe a number of factors are going to contrive to bring about its downfall in the years to come, among them the following:

1) As discussed in section 5, advances in technology, the increasing globalisation of financial markets and an expansion in the volume and complexity of tradeable financial instruments, together with what Alan Greenspan famously described as 'irrational exuberance' - and its opposite – are acting to make the system ever more sensitive at a time when we need it to be exhibiting more stability.

2) The financial crisis and its aftermath have laid bare modern Capitalism's greatest illusion, namely that one really can create a lot from a little with minimal long term investment. Instead, today's Capitalism is revealed to be far more effective as an agent that drives polarisation in the distribution of wealth than it is as an agent for delivering increasing wealth for all. The past decade in particular could be characterised as a period in which a few made a lot, a lot made only a little, and taxpayers were required to subsidise systemic failure on a grand scale.

3) Capitalism thrives on the flaws in human nature, and those flaws have found greater cultural expression in recent years. Short-termism, the need for instant

gratification and a focus on self have all grown in their influence as defining characteristics of our modern society. But a socio-economic backlash has begun, and as the constraints of earthly reality begin to bite this seems likely to gather momentum.

4) Capitalism's focus is on short term profit, and this is being increasingly derived at the expense of the long term greater good. It has perpetuated because people are reluctant to make short term sacrifices for long term benefit even when they know the consequences of not doing so may be dire, and has been aided by successive Governments' reluctance to focus adequately on objectives whose costs or benefits fall beyond the present electoral cycle. This was only ever likely to change when the cost of neglecting the long term greater good started to encroach on everyone's short term consciousness - and this is exactly what is now happening, as some of the threats mentioned in section 5 are beginning to bring bad news within reach of everyone's event horizon.

5) Population growth, dwindling resources and polarisation in the distribution of wealth will combine to ensure that excess in all its guises is going to become increasingly unfashionable in the years to come. A sea-change in attitude is underway and Capitalism, as a system characterised by excess (its central principle being that whatever profit has been banked in the past must, through the mechanism of economic growth, always be improved upon in future), is going to fare badly in the age of austerity that now awaits us.

6) Capitalism's disregard for, and inability to value, any interests beyond the corporate render it powerless to provide answers to any questions that corporations have no interest in asking. Unfortunately, virtually all the big challenges we now face transcend the boundaries of corporate interest. The key questions of tomorrow will not be how to achieve growth and make more money, but how to confront global threats and avoid societal collapse. These are questions to which Capitalism, so much a contributor to the problem, has no answer.

7) Capitalism is as reliant on increasing consumption as the World's economy presently is on oil. Both these engines of growth are heading for the buffers, at speed.

8) The concept of wealth that Capitalism is built upon is no longer fit for purpose. In particular Capitalism's concept of wealth places no value on waking up each morning to survey something other than an environmental wasteland, and in consequence the system contains no effective control mechanism to prevent itself from delivering one.

One aspect any critique of Capitalism must consider is the extent to which the symptoms of Capitalism's dysfunction are reflective of flaws in the doctrine itself ('systemic') or of flaws in the way it is deployed ('cultural').

In that context, it is interesting to note that, while in the wake of the present financial crisis focus has largely been on modern Capitalism's *cultural* failings (the substance of 1-5 above), it is Capitalism's *systemic* failings (6-8 above) that are shaping up to sink it. Quite when this will be recognised, and whether it will allow sufficient time for some of the more destructive consequences to be averted, remains to be seen.

For anyone who prefers a more practical illustration of the degree to which the objectives of Capitalism can be at odds with the public interest, among the myriad examples I could mention I can think of few better than that provided by the Iraq war, where a feast of human misery ran alongside a state-sponsored Capitalist banquet, an economic boom built not just on greed and optimism, but on the rubble of so many wasted lives. And for those who prefer their examples of Capitalist excess cloaked in more familiar regalia, I suggest a fact-finding visit to Dubai might be informative.

Insight into some of the human frailties that exacerbate the weaknesses of Capitalism as an economic system is hardly new. John Kenneth Galbraith noted them back when the World last faced a financial crisis of this magnitude: "Inaction will be advocated in the present even though it means deep trouble in the future", he wrote, for the hope of an easy life "causes those who know things are going quite wrong to say that things are fundamentally sound" [4].

Rather earlier in proceedings, way back in 1759, Adam Smith linked human sentiment more strongly to the acquisition of wealth: "the disposition to admire, and almost to worship, the rich and powerful", he noted, is "the greatest and most universal cause of the corruption of our moral sentiments" [11]. Coming from a man often regarded as the founding father of modern economics, and perhaps the World's original free marketeer, that was quite an observation.

Looking at the events of the last few years, one can only admire how well these reflections have withstood the test of time. The human capacity to learn has not yet, it seems, translated into more effective curtailment of the flaws in human nature. And, lest we forget, those flaws are not solely the dominion of people outside the actuarial Profession.

Beyond reminding us all that some actuaries do end up running banks, events surrounding James Crosby's departure from the FSA are most revelatory for the insight they provide into the mechanisms by which Capitalism's ills spread their contagion. If the Government appointed Mr Crosby to the FSA specifically to stamp out the kind of breaches of good governance over which we are led to believe he presided during his tenure as Chairman of HBOS, while one might still question the wisdom of the appointment one could at least see some merit in it. Unfortunately all the indications are that this was not the case, and that he was appointed because a) on standard benchmarks of progress (ie how much profit did his company make, and how quickly) he'd been very successful and b) because he'd convinced enough people in positions of authority that he was a jolly good chap.

This is the capitalist way. People do well by conforming, and by delivering what they are paid to deliver. The means by which they do so counts far less than the end. Few questioned to what risks Crosby and his ilk might have been exposing their companies in delivering stellar growth, and it would seem that the few who did were not always thanked for their trouble.

That he was still appointed to so senior a position at the FSA hints at the power of relationships, and to the importance of form over substance. It also reveals that, in today's Financial Services industry, there is little difference in underlying values between the poachers and the gamekeepers, for the simple reason that they are largely the same people.

On a smaller scale this is a situation that many of us find ourselves confronted with from time to time. Conflicts of interest are a staple of our trade. Many of us are employed in roles that require us to alternate between poacher and gamekeeper, and at an individual level many of us with varying degrees of success manage to reconcile the two.

As a Profession we rely upon our much-vaunted long term perspective and moral backbone to convince others - and perhaps on occasion ourselves - that the exercising of an actuary's sound judgement in striking an appropriate balance between short term commercial interests and the long term public interest will not be prejudiced by something as transient as the pressures of his or her current job role.

Yet how comfortably does that notion sit with the concept of poacher turned gamekeeper, and to what extent does it influence the efficacy with which actuaries expedite that proportion of their Professional responsibilities that transcends the demands of their employer? Which parts of his purportedly very large brain did Mr Crosby rewire on joining the FSA, and how does such rewiring fit with the Profession's own view of its members' independence and objectivity?

Whatever the answers, and whichever view one subscribes to, for those who choose to look the evidence is compelling: whether you have a Professional qualification or not, if you chase wealth for too long it can corrupt your morality, and if you let your business relationships become too cosy they can compromise your judgement. With Fred Goodwin (qualified accountant) and Tony Blair (barrister) as such fine contemporary examples of each, I will note only that it would be unreasonable to expect members of the Actuarial Profession to be any more or less corruptible than those of any other.

Of Wealth and Wellbeing

As for the consequences of our collective preoccupation with acquiring wealth, what Adam Smith and, to a lesser extent, Galbraith were both born too early to witness was the impact that the mass creation of wealth would ultimately have on the fabric of society. In that respect, the Britain of today would make a good case study.

Harold Macmillan undoubtedly had a point back in 1957 when he told people that they had never had it so good. But if he were still around today he would surely need to recalibrate his benchmarks, so great has been the pace of change in the intervening years. Half a century on, I would make the superficially similar but fundamentally different observation that, if growth, consumption and the acquisition of wealth without regard for consequence are to be our measures, we are *never again* going to have it so good.

For today, as the greatest follies of Capitalism's encounter with human frailty play out right before our eyes, it is genuinely true that in a material sense most of us have never had it better. Indeed future generations may yet come to marvel at what we had, and despair at how little some of us seemed to appreciate it. For despite the fact that we have never had it so well, even before the present financial crisis turned the national mood sour it would have been a brave man or woman who made the parallel assertion that we have never been happier.

Why the disparity?

Two principal reasons, I think. Firstly, deep down, rather like addicts who can't kick their habit, many of us as consumers know that we are contributing to a bigger problem, but just can't help ourselves. Secondly, when it comes to the distribution of wealth, people also understand that it has never been so polarised. Or perhaps more pertinently our society has never so effectively manifested to so many just how polarised it is.

And this, the sociologists now tell us, is the rub: absolute wealth, it seems, is not the primary source of our well-being. Competitive primates that we are, it is our *relative* position in the social hierarchy that counts, and wealth just happens to be the rather dysfunctional gauge by which modern society induces us to measure it. With league tables published every year telling us just how well the 'best' are doing, those who choose this benchmark as the primary measure of their status are given reason to be perpetually disappointed with their lot.

Into this mix we must add another ingredient, one that is becoming increasingly important: Galbraith's notion of 'deep trouble' back in the 1950s had a rather different flavour to that of today, and Smith, true to his economic roots, spoke principally of monetary wealth. Our modern perspective on the deep trouble of tomorrow, as I reflected upon earlier, is rather clearer, rather less financially-based and in many ways rather more worrying than the kind that has ailed our sensitive financial system in the past. People are aware of it, and as anybody who has been under threat of redundancy will know, awareness of a problem without knowing its impact or how it will be resolved is in some ways the most disconcerting feeling of all.

In this case, however, the solution largely sits in society's collective hands. As wealth distribution statistics and trends make clear, Capitalism's benefits are accruing disproportionately to a minority, at the price of an ever-increasing burden of debt - both financial and otherwise - on the rest.

For these reasons change is upon us, and the primary agent of that change will be the move to a society whose concept of wellbeing places less emphasis on traditional financial measures (income, wealth, GDP etc) and more emphasis on 'quality of life' factors (health, environment, social stability, sustainability of lifestyle etc). Whether it will take another boom and bust or a profound external trigger to get us there remains to be seen, but the present financial crisis has undoubtedly helped to accelerate the thinking that will get us there. In its wake, people's tolerance of Governments – not to say Professions with a vested interest – who think it appropriate to allow financial markets to dictate policy instead of framing policy to make financial markets better serve the interests of society has also been pushed far closer to breaking point.

That breaking point will be reached when Capitalism's inability to answer the questions now being posed of it has unavoidably been recognised. When it is, the avaricious pursuit of wealth by a few will no longer be so readily accepted because it will be understood to be detrimental to the interests of the rest. In this changing climate, the public will gauge our Profession's public interest credentials not by how it describes them on its website but by how it positioned itself in the change debate, or indeed whether it was heard at all. In which respect, if the Profession continues to avoid taking opportunities to demonstrate the qualities and characteristics that differentiate it from industry stereotypes it should not be surprised to find itself judged by them.

In the mad scramble to accumulate wealth, too many have for too long allowed themselves to lose sight of the fact that the point of doing so is undermined if the only place it can be spent gets trashed in the process. It is a rather trite point, but I cannot help thinking that if more of the World's smart people had invested as much collective effort in making the World a better place as they have in making themselves better off, our collective future might by now be looking rather less bleak. On a smaller scale, I believe our Profession to have been guilty of the same prejudice in its outlook: in particular, if as a Profession we'd invested as much time and effort representing the wider public interest as we have in representing corporate interests I feel sure some of the scandals that have plagued our industry in recent years could have been averted.

In the minds of the public at large, the penny is now beginning to drop. A lack of Government moral authority, a lack of individual appetite for personal sacrifice and a lack of investment in developing a proper mechanism for recognising the true cost of the intangible liabilities in Global Plc's balance sheet may be limiting concerted action, but they do little to hide the scale of the problem. Those intangibles are increasingly making their presence felt, and in doing so they are underlining the need for us to take pre-emptive action. We should recognise that our present course is leading us not towards social stability and global prosperity, but towards social unrest and global conflict.

Defending the Indefensible

Defenders of the faith will of course say that if the public believes that Capitalism is failing, then democracy provides an opportunity for this state of affairs to be addressed

91

through the ballot box. I don't propose here to explore the many facets of that particular argument, but I will make the basic, if unoriginal, observation that most of those who lead our industries, most of those who exercise proprietary control over many of our media institutions and a good number of those presently in Parliament (of all mainstream political persuasions) are products of the very system that now fails us.

In section 2 I noted that the Financial Services industry's present generation of leaders were hardly the best-placed individuals to lead its restructuring into something less oriented towards making ever-increasing levels of profit and more oriented towards public service. The same argument applies here, on a bigger scale: those in government, industry and the media, whose reputations have been built and fortunes made by exploiting current ideology are likely to be among the last to accept its failure.

People's willingness to relinquish a belief system when confronted with evidence that undermines it is a function of many things. Intelligence and their position in society may be among them, but I venture to suggest that the scale of their investment in that belief system is the dominant factor. In that respect, if 40% of Americans can refute the basics of evolution despite overwhelming supporting evidence to the contrary and despite the fact that changing beliefs would have no detrimental impact on their career prospects or their earnings potential, we can be sure that a much higher proportion of politicians, business leaders and tabloid proprietors will refute the failure of Capitalism for as long as is practicably possible, precisely because they believe - in some cases quite rightly - that their moral authority and their earnings potential *do* depend upon it.

In such circumstances, the absence of an electable alternative built around a new vision should be seen as less of an endorsement of the present system and more as an indication of how many of those who presently lead us have tied their reputations to it.

What can we deduce from this? Well, while the comparison with Creationism in some ways may be an unfair one, it does serve to underline an important point, which is that when the mind is predisposed to believing something it can be far from balanced in its evaluation of the available evidence.

By way of illustration, witness this offering in the leading column of a recent edition of the Economist (November 7th 2009): 'Defending the benefits of globalisation…', it opined, among other things, 'requires defending the enormous benefits that Capitalism has brought the World since 1989'. It is Capitalism, the Economist tells us, that has been responsible for 'the 500 million people dragged out of absolute poverty into something resembling the middle class'.

While the basis of the article was a reflection on events subsequent to the collapse of the Berlin Wall (hence the reference to 1989, when a UK-centric view of similar persuasion would no doubt have chosen an inception date ten years earlier), the clear inference is that any alternative economic system we might have chosen to adopt over the same period could not have achieved as much, or more. Yet it should be clear, upon more than a moments reflection, that the real driver of such benefit as has been achieved in the last twenty years has come not from Capitalism but from globalisation, in the form of the downfall of protectionist regimes that has allowed the export of western societal values, reduced trade barriers and given the developed world expanded access to cheap goods and labour.

That we now ship our matches from China, fly our mange-tout from Kenya and import our waitresses from Poland may be seen by sympathisers of the Economist view as just another manifestation of Capitalist efficiency, but I struggle to see each as anything other than the direct consequence of an economic system that is only capable of valuing explicit short term costs and benefits in a World characterised by gross inequalities in the distribution of wealth.

The Economist's facile thinking is just another example of the prevalence of soundbites in modern discourse that I mentioned in section 5. If, for all our vision and analytical prowess, we as actuaries do not challenge such substitutes for reasoned argument, why would anyone else?

For what it's worth, then, to Smith's and Galbraith's observations of human nature I therefore add my own: that the capacity of otherwise intelligent human beings to think in small dimensions, or not at all, about large-scale problems, and thereby avoid confronting them, is humanity's greatest weakness.

Today, with the first green shoots of another destructive economic crop cycle already springing forth, in some respects radical change looks as far away as ever. There is certainly little sign, in the action thus far taken or in most of the ideas thus far being discussed, that anyone in a position of authority is yet, in public at least, prepared to confront the implications of our addiction or the 'deep trouble' we face, or drive the kind of changes needed to even begin to address them. Meanwhile, the window of opportunity for us to plan for any kind of manageable transition to a more sustainable vision is slowly closing.

All at Sea

Autumn 2010, and the good ship Freemarket Capitalism is entering the final stage of its maiden voyage.

As one almighty iceberg that nearly rent her asunder now recedes into the distance, She's patched up, the mighty turbines are turning again and it is full steam ahead as usual.

Down below in the Corporate Interest dining room, a sense of normality has returned. All the broken crockery has been cleared and replaced, the floor's been mopped, the piano is tinkling, good wine is flowing, power is restored and the chandeliers are sparkling once more.

Up on deck, a distinct chill fills the air. Some of the ship's crew stare into the darkness, feeling her cutting through the waves with renewed speed and pondering what might lie ahead. Full steam ahead again? Has the Captain taken leave of his senses?

Where are the people with the good night vision? Downstairs, taking dinner.

The crew are concerned, but they won't disturb the diners. No point in spoiling their evening. The food is good and they are once again indulging the decadence of it all.

Meanwhile, away towards the horizon a menace looms, cold, dark and still.

For all on board the party isn't quite over. But it soon will be.

A Professional Response

A metaphor of over-dramatic fantasy? Perhaps. Perhaps not. But the stakes could scarcely be higher, and if we wish to promote ourselves as experts in the field of risk management, having so little to say about so big a risk is a poor way of demonstrating it.

One would have thought that a Profession of such combined vision and intellect as our own might recognise this and be prepared to invest rather more of its own capital in articulating an alternative. Unfortunately, evidence to date suggests that the Profession still has rather less enthusiasm for developing a new vision than it does for exploiting the existing one. Beyond the requirements expected of those who employ the services of its individual members, the Profession's public service investment is minimal. Few actuaries are presently employed in the public sector and few actuaries presently invest much of their intellectual capital in support of the wider public interest cause, because most of us are quite happy to leave public interest issues that fall outside the confines of our TCF, CPD or PRE responsibilities for someone else to concern themselves with.

Thus are matters of wider public interest left for the Profession as a whole to defend. And for the reasons I explored in section 7, thus are they poorly represented.

Our society faces a stark choice: if we don't change our ways voluntarily, change of an altogether different kind ultimately looks likely to foist itself upon us anyway. Which of the two transpires, for the time being at least, still looks to be a matter of choice. And it *is* a choice that matters. For while *proactive* change has the potential to be managed, the sequence of events likely to accompany enforced *reactive* change could easily spiral out of control.

Which of these choices should be our preference is clear enough, but *who is to make wise those that we require to have wisdom?*

As trained Professionals we often like to believe that the kind of human frailties that fuel Capitalism's weaknesses don't really relate to us, but for anyone not blind to it there is a growing pile of evidence to the contrary. In its discourse the Profession always leaves me with the impression that it believes industry problems sit exclusively outside the ranks of its membership. In continuing to believe this (or at least in continuing to act as if it believes it), the Profession appears complacent and continues to equip itself poorly to manage the consequences of being proved wrong.

For frailties, inside and outside the Profession's ranks, are a fact of life. No amount of mandatory CPD is going to banish them, and no amount of wishful thinking is going to stop them on occasion from manifesting. The challenge is to ensure the consequences are contained by not letting them compromise big decisions or distort the bigger picture – a task not aided by the fact that many of those who utilise our services often appear to show little interest in the bigger picture themselves. Yet we need to be mindful that as members of a Profession our public interest obligations are more onerous than theirs

As individuals and as a Profession we still tend to regard the greatest risk management challenges we face as someone else's problem to address (Government or the FSA for example). We are hardly alone in thinking this: in a wider sense the scale and intractability of such problems leave many people feeling helpless, and on that scale the benefits of individual action often aren't perceived to offer sufficient recompense for the personal sacrifice involved.

It is this kind of thinking that, among other things, allows people to indulge a destructive economic model and a destructive financial system until *someone else* tells them that change is needed, or that leads us not to invest in exploring alternatives until *someone else* either requires us to do so or pays us to do so. But the fundamental flaw in this thinking is that the really big problems *belong to all of us*: neither Government nor regulators could solve them in isolation even if they were minded to.

Capitalism may yet be reformed, or not, before it is too late. But in the interim, as actuaries we face a choice. We could, within the current system and under current regulation, continue as individuals and as a Profession to fulfil our current obligations in our traditional low-key actuarial way. Or we could show some of the boldness and spirit of enterprise for which, as the current faculty President has noted, we are not presently renowned, by taking a lead in highlighting the flaws of the present system, proactively seeking opportunities to inform policy and promote reform before it is too late.

Whether one sees any merit in the Profession adopting a more progressive approach may depend on whether one's preference is to look to the past or the future.

Any historical perspective would find some justification for our reticence. For while our public profile may not have improved appreciably, few people would contest that collectively the last twenty years or so have largely been prosperous ones for the Profession, as we - along with many others - have benefited from growth in the Financial Services sector. In that context how discomforting might it now be for us to be seen pushing a change agenda with the express purpose of addressing fundamental flaws in the system that delivered it.

However a Profession with a strong, forward-looking agenda would recognise such historical baggage for what it is, and have the wisdom to admit what most politicians still do not: that the old vision is spent, the old model is bust, and that a new social contract underpinned by a new economic doctrine is required. We could also learn another lesson that appears lost on most of those who presently lead us: that contrition has its place, and might even be appreciated.

There is good reason to be fearful of what lies ahead, but shutting one's eyes and imagining a better view is hardly the best answer. While Gordon Brown et al spend our billions putting us back on the road to growth, old paradigms are demonstrably failing and society continues its march towards what may well prove to be a seminal tipping point.

Quite what consequence will flow from this point being reached is anybody's guess, but one should already be clear: relative to its position today, the Financial Services industry is not going to emerge favourably from the resulting change in priorities. While for many reading this paper that may not be a particularly palatable truth, maintaining a state of denial will not be conducive to achieving the best possible outcome from the aftermath for either the Profession or its membership.

In a wider context, moving to a new economic system will not be easy or without pain and embracing one will require a fundamental change in the mindset of many people. That much I believed long before I started writing this paper, and I am not expecting people to be convinced by the simple act of reading it. Rather than labour the point here, I offer up just two heresies for consideration, the eventual acceptance of which will I believe pave the path to a new way of economic life: (i) *it is okay if profits don't increase every year,* and *(ii) it is possible to live without economic growth and still lead a fulfilling life.*

I don't seek to trivialise the challenges of the journey, or the plight of many for whom economic growth appears to offer the only escape route from their predicament. That too will require a change in mindset, to one that doesn't regard the redistribution of wealth as anathema (and of course redistribution between nation states, in its more subtle and less politically-sensitive guises - through for example a falling exchange rate and the import of cheap goods and labour - is exactly what we in the UK have been witnessing). I merely note that I can see no viable alternative.

It is unfortunate that discussion of something as profoundly important as the economic doctrine upon which our society is based has become so politicised. Thus does reasoned debate about what is right and wrong often find itself prejudiced by tired arguments between right and left.

We have tried socialism, we have tried free market Capitalism, and New Labour has offered us a third way which has at times seemed like the worst of both. I happen to believe there is a fourth way that combines the *best* of both, but it will only be tenable when the above hypotheses are accepted, and when it has been recognised that the solutions to the big challenges that now confront us are not in the gift of Capitalism, the Financial Services industry of the free market to deliver. While none of the mainstream political parties are as yet offering an alternative based around such a vision, it is surely only a matter of time before one emerges.

Unfortunately, this is another subject that the Profession approaches with customary timidity and trepidation. Perhaps in deference to its potential political connotations or perhaps as a result of the Profession's narrow interpretation of public interest, the 'C' word is hardly ever mentioned, the inference being that the Profession will dance without question to Capitalism's tune for as long as good politic requires it to, regardless of the potential long term consequences of doing so.

I proffer the view that this mindset is insular and short-term not public interest-oriented and long term in its outlook. Has the Profession anything to say about this subject, or will it simply attempt to watch the next unfolding disaster from the same detached vantage point as it watched the last one?

I would like to be proved wrong, but I fear I already know the answer. Nevertheless, with a change in mindset and approach, even without breaching the confines of its diplomatic traditions the Profession could easily better orient itself to at least begin scaling the foothills of a reform agenda.

With a better understanding of the likely direction of change, there are a range of steps that the Profession could be take, from small-scale initiatives through to the kind of policy overhaul I am calling for, to demonstrate that it is forward-thinking and adaptable, not small-minded and hostage to its history. In the last section of this paper in particular I consider a selection of more topical, if in some cases quite radical, initiatives that might offer scope for the Profession to diversify its interests.

Less radically, there are a number of things that as the Profession could do without stepping much beyond the confines of its traditional interest areas to demonstrate its cognescence of the need to change with the times.

I explore two such suggestions in more detail below:

1) Profit-Related Pay

I believe our Profession should be taking the opportunity now to renounce profit-related pay for any of its members who work for any financial institution in a capacity that carries significant public interest responsibility (ie in effect, in any traditional actuarial role).

I advocate this for the following reasons:

1) It is a traditional requirement of our role that we balance the interests of shareholders and policyholders. Accepting incentive payments based on profit puts unnecessary pressure on our neutrality in exercising that judgement.

2) Even if in practice our moral backbone is strong enough to withstand that pressure, the financial crisis has ensured that this will not be the public's perception. Public confidence in our industry, and by association in us, has suffered considerable damage. As a Profession we cannot afford for it to be lost.

3) For our Profession to announce such a change in its policy at this time would strike a chord with public sentiment, and the gesture would be well received. As anyone who has been following media coverage of the crisis will know, there are plenty of people now questioning why bankers and financiers on good salaries should need bonus incentives to do a good job in the first place. There will be many more who would consider it particularly inappropriate for actuaries to be rewarded in this way, given the weight of public interest responsibility carried by the Profession.

4) Members of a Profession that prides itself on its integrity, standards, moral backbone and long term view really ought not to require a short term incentive scheme, and in the present climate might well be seen as compromising those standards in accepting one.

5) Given the correlation between risk and financial return, it ought not to be considered appropriate for anyone acting in the capacity of advising financial institutions on matters relating to the management of risk to have their remuneration linked to the company's financial performance.

6) Matters of corporate governance are now attracting more attention, and the Profession's current practice would make for a soft target.

7) If we aren't proactive in proposing such a change we may yet one day find it enforced upon us, just as a mandatory CPD requirement was. It would be far better for the Profession's image to be seen proactively responding to the changing tide rather than being dragged along by it.

2) Policy Group

With no disrespect to its members – I did volunteer my own services, incidentally – I do think the terms of reference of the Financial Crisis Working Group are symptomatic of our Profession's lack of ambition. Interestingly enough, I started writing this paper in the month that the Group was formed. With its wings suitably clipped by a restrictive mandate, nine months on the Group still seems to have little of any substance to show for its labours.

In consequence, and as I touched upon earlier, what passes for news in the Group's updates are such banalities as 'Australian counterparts want access to our discussion board' or the fact that someone had been invited to give a speech on the subject of 'the lack of common sense in risk management' (quite why the focus was on lack of common sense in this particular area when there seem to be so many others to choose from wasn't clear. Perhaps it has something to do with the Profession's growing enthusiasm for all things risk management these days).

In similar vein, in its recent response to the FSA's Discussion Paper 09/2 (A regulatory response to the Global Banking Crisis), the Profession commented that its response would 'focus on quantitative risk management' as this is 'the area where we believe the Actuarial Profession has most influence'. I beg to differ. I think the Profession chose to focus on this area a) because this is one area where passing comment is unlikely to involve offending the sensitivities of others and b) because the Profession sees risk management as a growth area (in which respect, incidentally, I would invite any actuary who shares this sentiment to read Dan Gardner's 2008 book on the subject, simply entitled 'Risk'. It is an interesting and enlightening read, not least because it explores facets of the subject that as actuaries we rarely concern ourselves with, and it highlights a number of glaring contradictions in our society's approach to managing risk that as actuaries we rarely comment upon).

A Profession with a more progressive agenda might have called the Financial Crisis Working Group the Financial *Reform* Working Group. This would at least have shown that the Profession recognises that change is necessary, that this change extends beyond just the need for better quantitative risk management, and that the Profession has a role to play in helping to drive the change agenda.

In a wider context, I note that the Profession, in common with Government, has a habit of setting up working groups with mandates that are remedial rather than preventative, after profound events have happened rather than in anticipation of them. It might be rather uncharitable to describe this as management by disaster, given that some events clearly cannot be anticipated, but this is sometimes how it looks.

Another feature of these groups, one characterised by the Financial Crisis Working Group, is that their mandates are typically introspective, focusing largely on their subject matters' impact on the Profession's activities, and not on public interest implications or questions of wider policy. Thus the FCWGs primary objective, as described on the Profession's website, is 'to provide information for members'.

It seems to me that this continuing focus on the inside story is constraining the Profession's influence. It also seems to me that there is enough risk and uncertainty now confronting us to keep any Crisis Group busy for years. I therefore propose that the Profession should consider setting up a semi-permanent Crisis Group (that might be more appropriately called a Policy Group), whose mandate is not just provide information to its members but to contribute to fulfilment of the Profession's long term public interest obligations, by:

(i)   Leading the development of a policy agenda that puts the Profession in the best possible position to pre-empt and contribute to the alleviation of high risk events *before* they happen, rather than simply analysing the wreckage afterwards; and

(ii)   Helping to inform and shape the Profession's position on the kind of public interest issues touched upon in this paper, with a view to raising the Profession's profile, building its influence and demonstrating that it has the ability and foresight to lead change instead of always appearing to be at the mercy of events

The Management of Risk

As one might expect in a time of financial crisis when important risks have been so manifestly badly managed, talk of risk management is presently all the rage.

Government is talking about it, the companies that employ us are talking about it, the regulator is talking about it – indeed our present regulatory framework is built around it - and of course as actuaries we are already well used to working with it. No doubt even the banking industry, whose risk management shortcomings will now long be remembered by all, is flush with Management Development courses that expound on it.

In theory all this plays to what we perceive to be an actuarial strength, and as I noted above it is clear from the amount of exposure given to the subject that the Profession sees it as such, and sees this as a growth area for its members.

Many of us have witnessed the recent increasing focus on risk management from close quarters. I for one have lost count of the number of different risk registers that have crossed my palm in the last few years, and much collective good work has been done by actuaries and others to manage and mitigate a wide variety of risks faced by the institutions that we serve.

The fly in the risk management ointment, however, is that it is the small minority of risks that we don't register or seek to manage that are shaping up to sink us. Reread the list of risks set out in section 5, and consider how little as a Profession we have to say about their management. Consider also the risks that our present economic model and financial system pose to global stability going forwards, how close that system came to financial meltdown in 2008, and how little the Profession has thus far had to say about that also.

Do we reserve comment because such risks appear particularly intractable, or because the companies who employ us have little interest in them, or because we cannot agree what to say (in which respect see the next section), or because we don't consider it to be our position to speak out?

Whatever the underlying reasons, the consequence should be clear: each time a big risk is seen to catch us out, it undermines our risk management credentials.

My own view is that years of corporate thinking have prejudiced the way we think about risks, to the point where we now struggle to maintain a balanced risk management perspective.

That prejudice has been driven by two principal influences: 1) the Profession's contribution to risk management is exercised largely through the activities of its individual members, and 2) our contribution to risk management as individuals is exercised largely through the activities and interests of the financial institutions that we serve. This leads us, both as individuals and as a Profession, to over-invest in the management of risks that *are* of interest to those who pay for our services, and under-invest in the remainder.

The significance of this is that the risks that now pose the greatest threat *do* largely fall outside the sphere of interest of those who employ us. The reason being that companies, are principally concerned with risks that pose a *relative* threat, i.e. risks that if realised could place the company at a disadvantage relative to its industry peers. Consequently, the kind of macro risks that might sink the industry as a whole, or the economy as a whole, are left for Government to worry about. It is this thinking that, among other things, allowed many banks to take the kind of risks that precipitated the present financial crisis. Where the big players led, others followed: as none wanted to miss out on the opportunity for profit and risk being accused of short-changing their shareholders, the herd instinct kicked in.

One doesn't need to be either a risk management expert or a member of a Profession that puts the public interest at the heart of all that it does to see that there is a problem. The risk management needs of corporate interests and the risk management needs of the public interest clearly overlap, but they do not match; and while the gap may be small in terms of number of risks it is huge in terms of potential impact. Moreover, if the evidence of recent years is to be our guide, it seems that Government has neither the collective wisdom nor the long term vision needed to bridge it.

Not only is the Profession well-equipped to assist in the task, but in theory one could argue it is committed by its own public interest obligations to do so. The Profession's public interest mandate extends beyond that of most of the corporations its members serve. While banks have an excuse for being concerned only with the interests of their shareholders and their customers, as a Profession we do not.

In practice, however, our contribution to public discourse on such matters has thus far been minimal. And for so long as the Profession's strategic focus continues to be on serving the needs of its individual members, who in turn focus largely on serving the needs of their employers, this seems unlikely to change.

I remind you: *"The Profession is passionate about identifying matters of public concern where our input and involvement can be of benefit to society"*. So says our website.

As actuaries, if the gap between our words and our public interest deeds wasn't damaging to our Professional reputation this might not concern us.

As members of the public, if Government and its agents were more effective at managing the kind of risks that corporate interests and ourselves largely ignore this also might not concern us.

Unfortunately, neither hypothesis is true. We should be concerned, both as actuaries and as members of the public.

The present climate presents the Profession with plenty of opportunities to begin to redress the balance. It would be in the Profession's – and everyone else's - long term interests for it to start taking some of them.

11.   Actuaries and the Media

As part of my research for this paper, I conducted a web search of news articles mentioning actuaries. 4,430 references came up, which seemed quite promising on the face of it.

Excluding the odd well-documented bad news story involving actuaries with which most of you will be familiar, the first two pages of links yielded the following: four references were from our own website. Three were recruitment & networking sites; one was an article on obesity; one was an actuary praising someone else; one was a proud parent extolling the virtues of their actuarial son; two genuinely did give positive profile to actuaries, one an article relating to events in 1850 and the other a Ways and Means' statement by the Chancellor of the Exchequer in 1874.

I didn't make it to page 3.

I don't suggest for a moment that this is a fair gauge of our wider presence in the media or the financial press, but I do think it gives a fair indication of our profile.

As for other gauges of our actuarial profile, mentions in the popular press are few and far between, and rarely flattering. In Robert Peston's book [8] , we do get a mention on page 218 when he turns to the subject of the erosion of pension benefits and the sizeable hole in pension scheme funding (no prize for guessing the flavour of that coverage). There is the occasional TV appearance by one or other of our number on current affairs programmes, offering an expert view on some topical matter relating to one or other of our traditional business areas. Overall, though, none of this amounts to a collective presence in the public consciousness that one could describe as anything other than 'minimal'.

While one could argue that a low public profile might actually confer some advantage at a time when our industry's reputation is so poor, there are three stings in the proverbial tail of our relative anonymity. The first is that it does not help the Profession to exert its influence, and thereby fulfil its vision or public interest mandate. The second is that the absence of any distinguishing comment serves only to make it more likely that the Profession will be judged on the same measure as the industry in which it operates, an industry whose reputation could scarcely been worse. The third, as I alluded to earlier, is that the absence of any positive profile for the Profession means that media coverage, on the rare occasions we attract it, will be for our individual failings rather than our collective contribution to public discourse.

Even among those for whom the term 'actuary' does mean something, we are variously seen as technical boffins who talk a different language, as financial experts who are paid a lot, number crunchers who look after insurance money and pension funds, people who work out how long you're going to live, or – that favourite of jibes – simply as people who found accountancy too exciting.

Even in benign times, these are not the kind of labels on which good reputations are built or influence is expanded. However these are not benign times, and at the negative end of the public opinion spectrum, fairly or otherwise there are those who see us as responsible for the failure of Equitable life, responsible for reduced payouts on their mortgage endowments, responsible for the hole in their pension fund and now, perhaps, even as complicit in the failure of some banks.

If public perception is to be a benefit to us rather than a millstone around our necks, we must start to find ways to proactively influence it for the better.

A New Deal

I don't claim any detailed knowledge of the means by which the Profession develops and manages its media relationships, but as a consumer I can at least bear witness to the end result - which is that for an organisation of 20,000 members the Profession seems to have a poor media profile, characterised by periods of little coverage and relative anonymity punctuated by the fallout from sporadic industry scandals.

Perhaps it has always been thus. Perhaps the only change is that there seem to be more industry scandals these days weighing on the liability side of our PR balance sheet, with positive coverage no more or less limited than it has always been.

It is now eighteen years since Eric Short published his paper on Actuaries and The Media [12]. Sadly for our Profession's journalistic links, 1991 was also the year Eric retired. At that time Eric had under his belt thirty years as an actuary and twenty years as a journalist. In short - no pun intended - he was rather better placed to offer a view on this particular subject than I am.

Earlier that same year the Planning Joint Committee of the Institute and Faculty had set out its strategic objectives in a paper entitled 'Strategy for the 1990s', one of which made the following bold commitment:

"We will work actively to educate and influence journalists to better understanding of the actuarial contribution"

Eric did note at the time that he was somewhat unclear as to who 'we' or what 'the actuarial contribution' actually were, and lamented that his forthcoming retirement might prevent him from ever finding out.

Eighteen years on, I doubt he would be any the wiser. It seems to me that much of the contextual comment in Eric's paper would be equally valid today. In terms of the Profession's public persona, little seems to have changed, other than that industry scandals seem to have become more frequent in the intervening years. If anything, the need for the Profession a) to have a message and b) to ensure that its communication is effectively managed has become an even more pressing priority.

If it is to place itself in a position to respond to that challenge, the Profession would seem to have a number of obstacles to overcome.

The Importance of Policy

Organisations that have a strong media presence almost invariably have a clearly defined policy framework around which that presence is built.

This much is intuitive: it is a lot easier for an organisation to proactively engage with the media if it has a clearly defined modus operandi. Such clarity of purpose also makes it much easier for an organisation to be responsive to high profile events, gauge the appropriateness of media comment and engage in public discourse on topical issues while the subject is still fresh in people's minds.

Unfortunately, the Profession's present policy framework is too woolly and the range of interests it endeavours to represent is too wide to provide such clarity of purpose.

Not only are public interest responsibilities loosely defined, but the circumstances in which the Profession might collectively deign to engage in discourse on any particular subject are also loosely defined. Obligations are nebulously worded and frequently followed by a suitably woolly 'where appropriate'. Furthermore the range of roles and responsibilities that actuaries undertake has broadened - rendering any representative formulation of policy position more challenging - and the current introspective strategic focus on supporting individual member needs reinforces the impression that the Profession attaches low priority to matters of collective policy and building its external profile.

The challenge is compounded by the Profession's desire to serve many interests, not all of them mutually compatible. Defining a policy framework is a lot easier if it can be aimed at a specific purpose: if a Profession seeks to serve both public and commercial interests, while maintaining relationships with government, regulators, industry bodies and the like, not to mention the minor matter of keeping its own members happy, it may leave itself little room for manoeuvre – not to say little scope for comment- if its primary objective is to keep all within diplomatic reach at all times.

If our Profession served *only* the public interest, I don't doubt that it would have been far more vocal on some of the pertinent issues that have made headlines in recent years – and who knows, it may have voiced concerns before some of them had even hit the headlines. That it didn't may be seen by some as expeditious deference on the part of the Profession to other interests, and by others as indicative of a Profession that is introspective in its focus and remote from the concerns of ordinary people.

Clearly there is a balance to be struck. The Profession cannot justify pursuing the public interest without regard for its members interests any more than it can justify pursuing commercial interests without regard for the public interest. However, while there may be no 'right' answer as to how that balance should be struck, my contention on the basis of events in recent years is that the Profession is getting that balance badly wrong, and that many people, fairly or otherwise, will be concluding from the Profession's lack of profile and lack of public discourse on pressing issues that it is pursuing commercial interests at the expense of the long term public interest.

If the Profession cares about its reputation, in today's climate whether there is truth in this observation matters less than the public's perception of it. More pertinently, history is littered with examples that clearly illustrate how the lack of timely intervention on matters of public interest tends to result in a worse outcome for all concerned in the long run, when the matter at hand later unravels in the public domain and on a bigger scale than it might otherwise have done had whistles been blown and the alarm been raised.

Given this, and given that our industry is now being scrutinised as never before, the case for the Profession to review and clarify its policy in this area has never looked stronger. Such a review could serve to restore better balance to the efficacy with which the Profession pursues its public interest mandate and provide the clarity of purpose needed to enable the Profession to be more responsive to events in the outside world.

Reaching for Consensus

Even if the Profession is able to articulate more clearly the interests it represents within a more definitive policy framework, and even if the Profession's leadership is able to demonstrate the boldness and spirit of enterprise required to implement it, this will count for little if the Profession cannot find a more efficient means of reaching consensus.

Before the merger debate came along to dominate the Profession's consciousness, I suspect more than a few members of the Profession were unfamiliar with the nuances of Institute and Faculty voting rules, and in the case of the Institute might have thought that a 70% vote in favour of a particular course of action would be enough to carry it. I for one would have presumed as much. Not so, as we are all now aware.

The merger process has also highlighted that there are those in the Profession who would wish their opinion to count on each and every subject that the Profession might be minded to express a view on. That being the case, under present voting rules it seems unlikely that there would be any subject of topical interest upon which the Profession would be able to agree a position on any timescale short enough for it to capture an audience.

Thankfully we do not have to have a vote on everything that the Profession chooses to say, but I am still left with the discomforting feeling that this is at least in part why it *has* so little to say.

Indeed 'paralysis through lack of consensus' might be a good description of the Profession's condition over the last year or so. What is not so clear is the extent to which that condition is impacting upon the conduct of the Profession's day-to-day business. No examples spring to mind in recent years for the question to seem anything other than hypothetical, but let us imagine that a situation arose where the Profession really *did* want to make some meaningful contribution to public discourse on a contentious matter of considerable public interest. How, given its present policy framework and obligations to members, would it decide what it was going to say? How many recognised industry 'names' would need to dissent on any proposed line in order to render the Profession mute? Would just the *thought* that they might be enough to render it mute?

I don't know the answer to these questions, but I do think that they are relevant, and like anyone else I can bear witness to the end result. Which is that on present form the Profession could scarcely be less effective in its public discourse even if it *were* mute, and could scarcely be less effective in its decision-making even if its individual members could veto anything.

Furthermore, while I do not question that a merger between Institute and Faculty would have removed one of the obstacles on the road to finding a common voice, on present evidence it is difficult to be optimistic that a merger would not simply replace two near-invisible organisations with one.

Progress of sorts, perhaps, but the fact is that in today's fast-changing world, if the Profession is to play a leading role in the change debate it will need to demonstrate far more fleetness of foot and have a far clearer sense of purpose and direction than has hitherto been required of it.

The benefits of a stronger presence should be clear. In the present climate disillusionment is rife, and bad news showers down like confetti. The public long for a voice that better represents their interests, but they are not hearing one. Yet here we are, a Profession that is supposedly passionate in its commitment to defend the public interest, and we have little of any consequence to say.

In his 1991 paper Eric spoke of the need for actuaries to educate journalists, but in the intervening years tectonic plates have been shifting. These days, few media commentators would be minded to take lessons from representatives of the Financial Services industry whether they are actuaries or not. Yet in a wider sense people need educating more than ever about the choices that now confront them.

In the climate of today there are precious few with a voice independent enough or authoritative enough to assist with that education, so disrespected have the traditional instruments of business and state now become. The Profession could gain considerable benefit from this situation, if only it could bring itself to speak. If the Profession could find the boldness to make an impression, there has surely never been a better time for it to do so.

Not all journalists seek to revel in our industry's failings. Deep economic crises, like wars, tend to unite people behind a common cause. While the level of trust among many journalists and their readers that either our present generation of politicians or the Financial Services industry are fit to serve the long term public interest may never have been lower, we all at least have a shared interest in finding the best means of ensuring that in future both do.

There are good and bad journalists just as there are good and bad actuaries, of course. But the truth is that the better-educated and better-informed elite among media commentators often seem to have a far clearer grasp of priority and public mood than many of those who speak for Government or our own industry sometimes do.

The downside, of course, is that all journalists, good and bad, are always tuned into what is newsworthy. Their priority is to sell copy, not to pursue public interest – and for all the overlap between the two, as the feeding frenzy over MPs expenses demonstrated only too well the media's response to events does not always act in the interests of a balanced public interest debate.

This misalignment of media interest and public interest does not alter the fact that a number of finance correspondents, particularly those writing for the quality broadsheets, are heavily involved in leading the change debate and driving new thinking. For unlike Government and many in our own industry, they can afford to be less deferential to commercial interests, and their careers and reputations do not require them to defend failing paradigms.

No surprise, then, that most of the voices that warned of forthcoming financial crisis came from this select group, and no surprise that Government and those who lead our own industry largely ignored them or, worse, on occasion sought to discredit them.

If the Profession wants to build its reputation and its profile, these are the kind of people that it should be engaging with. Moreover if the Profession is true to its own public interest ideals and its purported long term perspective, it will recognise that it shares the same goals, for we all have an interest in working towards a more sustainable future than the one into which our present socio-economic model is leading us.

For the Profession to exercise any influence in this respect will not only require greater clarity of purpose, direction and policy, but also more effective collective media representation by the Profession as a whole. Which in turn leads back to a need for the Profession to not only conduct a review of its strategic priorities and direction, but also to address the issues with its constitution that the merger process has served so effectively to highlight.

Closer to home, at a time when traditional business areas are being squeezed, the Profession will need to diversify its interests if it is to continue to prosper in the world of tomorrow. As our recent history has shown, that is difficult to achieve when the

Profession has so limited a profile. A stronger, more effective media presence could do much to assist.

Does our Profession have the appetite to overcome these hurdles, rebuild its reputation and increase its public profile in this way? If it doesn't not only will a big opportunity at a critical time to contribute to the greater public good have been missed, but the notion that the World is ever going to realise how much it needs actuaries is surely going to ring increasingly hollow.

On the presumption that the Profession does wish to expand its influence and does want to find ways of addressing the issues that presently prevent it from doing so, I turn now to what the future might hold, and how if it is capable of adapting the Profession could prosper.

12. Actuaries and the Future

Given the many and varied challenges faced by today's society, with our intellect and skill set there really ought to be no reason for any actuary to be unemployed. But if our Profession's policy of tomorrow continues to mirror its practice of today, it may yet create one.

I noted in section 5 that globalisation had until the events of last year been quite kind to Britain, at a time when there is much evidence to suggest that our global economic system is being rather less kind to the planet as a whole.

As I have sought to explore in these pages, I believe we are now witnessing the beginnings of a backlash on both counts, one that will see a dramatic change in priorities and one whose long-term impact will be profound. Quite how much collective pain we will all have to endure before a new order emerges remains to be seen, and may well depend on the extent to which pre-emptive steps are taken to mitigate the worst of the consequences before they actually happen.

In that respect, past precedents are not encouraging. But while Government and industry leaders pursue an agenda based on as quick a return as possible to business as usual, an increasing number are now asking wider questions about where all this is leading us.

The underlying reason for this change in sentiment is that in recent years the gap in ideology between quick fixes and long term solutions and between economic fantasy and earthly reality has been steadily growing into a stretch of precipitous proportions. The days of any Government – or for that matter any Profession with long term public interest obligations - being able to straddle that gap without suffering a fall are surely numbered.

The ultimate outcome seems clear: one way or another the World economy in general, and the British economy in particular, is going to have to be restructured into something that is far less damaging to the long term prospects of its citizens.

Elsewhere in this paper I have touched on some of the things that I believe we could be doing now, both individually and as a Profession, not just to help better prepare for that change but to begin demonstrating that we are cognescent of the need for it, so I won't repeat them here.

However, if our Profession is to stand any chance of fulfilling the bold visions painted for it by successive leaders of both Institute and Faculty, and if it is to actively contribute to change rather than simply avoid being left stranded by it, such steps in isolation will not be enough.

The Challenges Ahead

Nobody knows for sure when the oil will run out; nobody knows when the impact of global warming will really begin to bite or quite how bad its effects will be; nobody really knows where the scramble for dwindling resources will lead us; nobody really knows what chain of events the impact of these or the other big risks I've touched upon in this paper would unleash.

In light of such uncertainty, speculation on specifics is fruitless. Predicting the future is difficult enough in benign socio-economic times. Doing so as the World enters a period of great turbulence is a task best left to fools and gamblers. But I would urge the Profession to at least recognise that a period of great change is now upon us.

If one believes that the past is still a guide to the future, and if one believes that the events of the last twelve months or so represent little more than a one-off outlier, it is possible to believe that we can continue to prosper by continuing to chart our present course. In present circumstances, however, to believe either hypothesis is an act of considerable faith. With the World's economy entering uncharted waters, it is a central tenet of this paper that such faith represents dangerously complacent thinking that the past is no longer a guide to the future, and that one way or another wide-ranging socio-economic reform is now inevitable.

As reality begins to bite and the scale of our predicament becomes increasingly apparent, opinions seem likely to polarise. Those whose interests and reputation are heavily invested in old paradigms will no doubt resist change to the last, while support for those of more progressive outlook will continue to grow. Such middle ground as there is will continue to shrink until it is little more than a sharp fence, one that our Profession, in its customary eagerness not to offend any of its conflicted interests, may yet find itself impaled upon.

Only when our society finds a more balanced set of priorities, develops a less financially-oriented concept of wealth and adopts an economic model less driven by the quest for ever-increasing profit will our Profession be able to serve all those interests without contradiction. In the meantime, the Profession will be fooling few other than itself if it thinks that a strategy based on promoting members interests, who in turn invest the vast majority of their time supporting commercial concerns, is in any meaningful way promoting the long term public interest.

The day before the event that precipitates this change, the opinions of those with influence will no doubt divide as they always have: broadly speaking, there will be those who were seen to be leading calls for change, there will be those who were seen to be resisting change, and there will be those who chose not to be seen at all.

In this scenario it wouldn't be just individuals who found themselves judged harshly in the wake of events. Institutions and organisations with public interest obligations who find themselves on the wrong side of progress, from political parties to Professions, may well feel the hand of history weighing heavily on their shoulders too.

How, in such a reckoning, do you think today's Actuarial Profession would fare?

On present form, I think I can safely note that few people outside its ranks would be crediting it of leading new thinking. And while in the wake of the present financial crisis 'nobody saw it coming' has proved a multi-purpose fig leaf behind which many of those who should have known better have been able to hide their embarrassment, when *real* change comes to pass pleading ignorance of the underlying risks and issues is unlikely to be seen as a convincing defence. And it will look particularly weak when offered by a professional body that has been trading on its risk management credentials

This is the direction in which the Profession's present strategy is leading it. Today's Profession prefers change by osmosis: train individuals with the basic toolkit, ensure that they meet their ongoing CPD requirements and let their own boldness and spirit of enterprise take care of the rest.

Osmosis does work, to a point. Over the last twenty years or so, actuaries have steadily seeped into the fields of general insurance and investment. A few others have found their way into banking, with - I'll be charitable - mixed results, and latterly, in the Profession's customary low-key way, moves have been made to facilitate a similarly steady seep into the field of wider risk management.

Notwithstanding these gradual changes, however, the Profession's interests remain largely confined within the cell walls of its traditional business areas. Osmosis is not an effective agent of change, for the simple reason that it tends to finds itself subsumed by greater forces.

For many who join the Profession, actuarial careers can have a habit of becoming locked-in at quite an early stage. Switching between disciplines even within our traditional business areas requires effort, and while some actuaries do occasionally make the switch between areas, for example from life to general insurance or from pensions to investment, the vast majority do not. In an industry of burgeoning complexity, this trend has perhaps been reinforced by the perceived value of having a specialism. Many of us, from an early actuarial age, are encouraged to 'find our niche'.

While from both an individual and an industry perspective there is some value in this, it can also be something of a limiting dynamic. It is limiting in the sense that it acts to inhibit our adaptability to change, it acts to reduce opportunities for us to gain and maintain a wider industry perspective, and it makes it more difficult for the Profession to either break into or build its reputation in wider fields.

Given that movement is limited even between disciplines within our traditional business areas, it is hardly surprising that the Profession as a whole has struggled to expand its influence outside those areas. For the leaders of our Profession to call for greater boldness and spirit of enterprise is laudable, but it misses the point that if the Profession is to expand its influence it is the Profession *as a whole* that will need to take a lead in demonstrating those qualities.

Why? Because human nature being as it is, individual enterprise more frequently finds expression in the pursuit of individual ambition than it does in the pursuit of collective good.

In actuarial terms, *in general* this translates into proportionately more investment by individuals in activities that they perceive will promote their own career development (usually by devoting the bulk of their rime to serving priorities set by their employer). When it comes to finding a little more margin in our bases, eking out a little more profit, making our products and services a little more tax efficient, finding creative ways of transferring risk or helping to design complex investment products, for example, our degree of enterprise as individuals can be truly impressive. Many a successful actuarial career has been built on it. But how much of our individual enterprise presently finds expression in ways that promote either the longer term interests of the Profession or the wider public interest?

Most of us recognise that Lord Turner's recent observations about the social worth of some financial sector activities are valid, even if some might choose not to admit it. What many might be more reluctant to concede, however, is that his comments could be just as appropriately used to describe some elements of a typical actuarial job description these days. For in truth much of our creativity, as presently expressed, has little influence on the forces that shape the public's opinion of what we do and how valuable it is perceived to be. It is not the kind of enterprise or endeavour that has profile beyond the boundaries of those who employ us, and it is not the kind of enterprise that will convince a sceptical public that it needs us.

What the public might value more is actuaries who as individuals have an independence of mind that is less compromised by, and more challenging of, the demands of their employer; actuaries who are motivated to serve the wider public interest with the same degree of enthusiasm that they serve their own interests or those of their employer; actuaries who bring more imagination to what they do, and who are more imaginative about what they could do; actuaries who spend less time grappling with short term problems and more time developing long term solutions; and last but not least, they might place greater worth on a Profession whose voice is more commensurate with its vision, one that lives up to its public interest billing.

To date, while in recent years the Profession's difficulty in giving tangible substance to its public interest obligations may have extracted a reputational price, it has not really hit the Profession where it hurts. M&A activity, industry consolidation, changes in regulation, the pensions revolution, dealing with the fallout from legacy systems and just keeping hold of the financial reins in an increasingly complex financial world have kept most of us plenty busy without the need to extend ourselves far beyond the boundaries of our traditional roles. In similar vein, while the changing perceptions of our industry have hardly helped the Profession extend its influence, neither do they appear thus far to have had any significant detrimental impact upon its collective workload.

Reflect, though, on the peculiar confluence of factors that has been keeping us all busy, and consider the likely trend in each. Yet more regulatory change may again be upon us, but it cannot last forever. People's trust in institutional investors as guardians of their savings, their mortgage endowment or their pension plan has been seriously undermined. Our industry is ripe for a shake-out, the tax system is ripe for simplification, and M&A activity offers no long term solution even if levels do pick up again as we emerge from recession. Into that mix add the current public perception of the industry as a whole and the long term tightening of fiscal belts that will soon begin hitting people's pockets. And last but not least, factor in the impact of a likely fundamental shift in society's priorities, away from an obsession with wealth accumulation and towards finding a sustainable mode of existence. Reflect on all this, and ask yourself how reliable our industrious past is as a guide for our future.

The last point above is particularly pertinent. The Financial Services landscape itself is in the process of changing, and the ultimate result, if pursuit of the Greater Good is to eventually prevail, will be a smaller, simpler and more sensibly-rewarded Financial Services industry. This will happen because the public interest *needs* a smaller, simpler and more sensibly-rewarded Financial Services industry, and needs some of the intellectual resource currently subsumed to it to be deployed in rather more effective ways to solve rather more pressing problems.

I don't expect many in our industry or our Profession to endorse that view. I don't even expect the Profession to discuss the prospect, though in the interests of honest and open debate I would of course urge it to.

Looking ahead to this time of more balanced priorities, there will surely still be a need and healthy demand for banking, finance and insurance services. Moreover the need for continuing actuarial support in our traditional areas also looks assured. But we need to be realistic in our assessment of where the industry is heading, and of the likely impact this will have on the demand for traditional actuarial resource.

Opportunities for Actuaries in a Changing World

Ours is the Profession that takes a long term view, ours is the Profession with expertise in risk management and financial analysis, and ours is the Profession that is passionate about its pursuit of the public interest.

This is not what others say about us. It is what we say about ourselves.

If the Profession can find a means to strike a more ethical balance in the investment of its resources between the pursuit of commercial interests and the pursuit of the Greater

Good, there are many areas of public interest that could benefit from the application of such vision and skills.

The examples I include below were chosen not for their proximity to our traditional areas of responsibility or the ease with which the Profession could expand into them, but to illustrate the range of opportunities that might be open to a Profession that was more passionate about the public interest and had a less blinkered World view. I would also venture to suggest that most of them represent rather more pressing needs than some of the activities that presently occupy our time.

1) Actuaries Can Do Banking (and should)

Actuaries have long been familiar with the concept of analysis of surplus. But others in the financial sector, it seems, are not. That at least would be the conclusion one would draw based on the recent experience of the banking sector.

If banks are to continue to be allowed to have a hand in both the casino and the high street, as looks increasingly likely, can we at least have better information made available to us about the respective sources of their profit? Can we see how much is derived from retail banking, currency speculation, mortgages, insurance, SIV trading, corporate lending etc. Let's also see how much capital is notionally allocated to each, together with the supporting risk analysis, and let's see the corporate bonus pool as a percentage of payroll split into the same categories. And let's see it published annually, in a prescribed format, for every large financial institution, and certainly for every institution that we as taxpayers have a financial stake in.

At the time of writing, UK taxpayers' collective investment in the banking system amounts to around £180 billion, or around £3,000 per head of population. UKFI, the company set up to look after that interest for us, has just 15 employees. Its business to date has been conducted largely behind closed doors, which is disconcerting given the scale of investment they are representing on our behalf.

Banking has become far more complex than it ought to be or needs to be to serve the interests of its customers. For every actuary that might manage a bank badly there are plenty more who could bring valuable financial and risk management insight to bear in helping to ensure that banks are better managed to the benefit of all. Perhaps it is time we stopped hiding behind the notion that actuaries do not do banking and started lobbying Government, regulators and the banks that employ some of us to utilise our skills to better effect in what is evidently a critical risk area. For as we have learned to our cost, these days we are *all* doing banking, whether we want to or not.

2)   Economic & Financial Market Reform

Capitalism's failings as an economic doctrine are beginning to cost us dearly. No amount of numerical dexterity is going to make economic growth + population growth + resource consumption equate to a sustainable future. Instead of acquiescing when others persist in trying to defy this reality, the Profession could better serve the public interest by promoting reasoned debate on the subject, with the aim of helping to develop a sustainable Plan B before it is too late.

The Profession could be making a far more effective contribution to the ideological debate about what kind of economic and financial market reforms are now needed. What does the Profession think of the fitness of today's financial markets to withstand the challenges of tomorrow, or the FSA's Tobin Tax proposals, or of the social value of the various types of transaction that characterise today's financial markets? What ideas does it have to help mitigate some of the influencors of the trend towards increasing volatility I listed in section 5? The regulator has expressed a view, Government has expressed a view, and if we are as passionate about the public interest as we say we are, so should we.

3)   Public Sector Reform

As mentioned earlier, the notion that the public sector is riddled with inefficiency has been with us for so long that it has increasingly come to be accepted by many as a fact of public sector life. Successive Governments have had little impact on the problem; indeed one could argue that continual changes in political masters have served only to compound it.

Given the present fiscal situation, whichever party wins the next election is going to need to find big savings from the public purse. Individual taxpayers have nobody to properly represent their interests in this respect, as history has shown us that successive Governments are often either conflicted by the principle or ineffective in their approach to tackling the problem (or both). As a Profession and as an industry we invest proportionately far too much time concerning ourselves with how to assist our clients reduce or avoid payment of tax and far too little time in shedding light on the efficacy with which it is being spent.

The issue of public sector efficiency transcends party politics, or at least it ought to. The sector costs us all as taxpayers a small fortune each year. Perhaps it is time it was opened up to more insightful analysis and more independent scrutiny. I noted earlier that public sector problems are more about quality of management and quality of information than they are about quality of people. The Profession's toolkit and public interest mandate equip it well to assist, and doing so would strike a populist chord. It would be a bold move, but in the present fiscal climate if the

Profession could find an effective mechanism by which to offer its services it would be difficult for any party of Government to refuse.

4) Private Finance Initiatives

Bank bailouts notwithstanding, any initiatives our cash-strapped Government has to fund that look like they could offer a financial return to someone tend these days to be sourced through Private Finance Initiatives (PFIs). Some 640 PFI contracts have been signed by Government in the last twelve years, committing the taxpayer to over £200 billion in repayments over the next decade. Unfortunately these deals don't always end up offering good value to the taxpayer, partly because the tender process has become increasingly politicised and partly because treasury officials and Government departments aren't always effective in their evaluation or management of the initiatives.

Perhaps there is an opportunity for a commercially-minded Profession well-versed in the art of analysis and financial management to help. It would certainly be in fitting with our public interest mandate, and it might even be in our own interests as taxpayers for our services to be offered to Government at a discounted rate.

5) Pensions Reform

Another good place to start looking for public sector savings might be in the public sector pensions provision. It would be interesting to see an analysis of that provision across the public sector in comparison with its equivalent in the private sector (based, say, on FTSE 100 companies), with particular focus on the relative cost of each, and how this has changed over the last twenty years or so. Who better placed than our own Profession to undertake such a study, in the wider public interest?

6) Policy Initiatives

Many of the large-scale problems we presently face require pre-emptive measures to be taken now to mitigate against adverse consequences in the future. This is essentially risk management on a scale that transcends corporate boundaries in pursuit of a greater good.

Unfortunately Government has a track record of doing this poorly, and industry has a track record of doing it hardly at all. We could do much to enhance our own risk management credentials by being more proactive in promoting public debate and formulating policy initiatives in some of these areas (economic reform, population growth, the management of scarce resources etc).

7) International Collaboration

Global problems, from tax havens to financial crashes to radical overhaul of economic systems to global warming to energy crises, demand global solutions. Governments understand this, but when the chips are down they still tend regularly to slip back into short term thinking and pursue national interests at the expense of collaboration.

In a global context the UK Actuarial Profession's reputation has arguably fared rather better than that of either the UK Government or the UK Financial Services industry in recent years. Moreover in actuarial terms the UK Profession has proportionately more influence and genuinely global reach. As such, if it had the will to do so the UK Profession could be doing far more to promote stronger working relations with its international counterparts, joining forces to help formulate policies to tackle global risks, and helping to bring co-ordinated pressure to bear on Governments around the world to collaborate in dealing with matters of urgent global concern.

8) Tax Reform

It is widely accepted that the UK's system of taxation is inadequately targeted, over-complex and in need of an overhaul. The actuarial and accountancy Professions have considerable expertise in this area, if only through having invested so much effort in identifying opportunities to exploit it to their clients and customers advantage. As such the Profession is well placed to help inform a new, more transparent system of taxation that better serves the long term public interest.

9) Renewable Energy and Recycling Policy

Investment in each of these has fallen on hard times recently. Thanks to the financial crisis and the associated collapse in oil prices, investment in renewables has taken a nosedive since early 2008, at a time when it should be being massively expanded. Similar logic (if one can call it that) explains a reduction in investment in recycling. Could the Profession not bring its risk analysis and projection skills to bear in articulating a longer term business case based on a more realistic economic cost/benefit model? That oil might run out looks rather less a one in 200 year risk than a one in fifty year near-certainty, particularly if fears that key producers may have been over-estimating their reserves prove well-founded. Is it not time we dedicated more of our long term vision and risk analysis ability to the task of painting some of the scenarios that could arise from underinvestment in these areas, given their criticality to the long term public interest?

10) Transport policy

One doesn't need to look beyond the relative cost of road, rail and air travel, and how the cost of each has changed over the last twenty years, to see that our transport policy is a mess. Furthermore Governments that talk green while expanding airports and building more roads do little to reassure that the issue is in safe hands.

Little short of a fundamental overhaul of travel taxes and incentives and a new financial framework for properly evaluating the respective costs and benefits of different modes of transport is needed. The actuarial skill set is well-suited to the task of helping to building one, and the Profession could also bring a much-needed independent and objective view to a subject that has become something of a political football.

11) Carbon costing

One of the largest and most topical intangibles on the World Plc balance sheet, this is becoming a big employer. The development of reliable carbon models is growing in importance as the scale of the global warming challenge becomes clearer. Actuaries are well-qualified to provide input both into modelling techniques and to support analysis and projection of long term costs and benefits.

12) Food labelling

We've got used to eating what we like when we like, but if an enforced drastic change in habits is to be avoided we are going to need to be a lot smarter about the balance between consumption and conservation than we presently are. It will be necessary to introduce far more effective labelling and pricing of foodstuffs before as consumers we are able to make informed choices and pay a price more reflective of the true resource cost of what we eat and drink. This will require complex modelling of many inter-related factors, for example energy invested in production vs energy value on consumption, amount of land required for production, for how long it is required and with what environmental impact, etc. Again, the analytical and modelling skills of actuaries would be well-suited to assist with this.

Many will no doubt recoil in horror at the notion of actuarial involvement in some of the areas I mention above. Some of the later entries in particular are a full spectrum away from our traditional interest areas. I am not suggesting for a moment that the Profession should seek to embrace them all even if its investment would be welcomed - and in some cases doubtless it wouldn't. But if the Profession is to be seen as a force for good in a brave new World, these are the kind of initiatives it would help for it to be seen supporting. They are also the kind of initiatives that the World desperately needs to be supported.

It may be an inconvenient truth, but the big challenges we now face are being largely ignored by corporate interests and routinely mismanaged by Government. While there may be no obligation on our Profession to help fill the gap, I believe that the Profession's underinvestment in the public interest element of its balance sheet is becoming acute. If there is a central theme to this paper, it is that the Profession and the wider public both have an urgent need for that balance to be redressed.

The unstated challenge is that in this warped economic system of ours serving the wider long term public interest rarely offers financial rewards commensurate with those on offer for servicing corporate interests, a situation whose consequence is compounded by the detrimental impact the short term preoccupations of the latter are now having on the former.

The Profession as a whole could be doing more to help redress the balance by better supporting activities that contribute to the wider public interest. Recognising that the commitment of resource requires funding, in response to the recent increased revenues derived from other activities (notably mandatory CPD), instead of reducing membership contributions would it not be better for the surplus to be invested in supporting initiatives that might help raise the profile of the Profession in the public consciousness? I mentioned earlier that mandatory public service would be a far better investment on the part of the Profession than mandatory CPD. If as a Profession we were committed to that cause there are a number of mechanisms through which such an investment could be effected.

In the absence of a new economic system that strikes a better balance between reward and contribution, and in the absence of any commitment from the Profession as a whole to serve the wider public interest, the question that poses for each of us as individuals is to what extent we are prepared to compromise our earnings potential for the pursuit of a greater good. To what extent is supporting a more worthy cause sufficient recompense for a drop in our income? What price a sustainable future, and what price our assistance in helping society to build one?

To those who would baulk at the notion of taking a pay cut in order to better serve the public interest, I would note that in the new World in which we are soon likely to find ourselves, demand for our traditional services is going to reduce. That means if we do not find new interest areas, if actuarial unemployment is not to rise then actuarial pay is likely to reduce anyway.

To those who view a move to support such initiatives as a radical step away from our traditional business areas and a dilution of the application of our core actuarial training, I also agree - but with a caveat. Clearly much of what we do as actuaries in our traditional areas of responsibility is valuable and technical work, but consider also how much of our time is spent in playing the corporate game, dealing with general matters of business governance and corporate management, helping those who employ us to squeeze out a little more market share or a little more margin, endlessly chasing competitive advantage in ever more ingenious ways, tweaking products, fine-tuning bases, ticking regulatory boxes or simply coping with increasing complexity. Such activities also represent a rather tenuous application of our actuarial training, and in comparison with some of the alternatives in which it could be invested they also represent a poor return on our intellectual capital.

To those who view that it is not the responsibility of actuaries to tackle such problems, I agree, to a point. If others were doing a better job of representing the wider public interest in all its guises, I might agree more. But would they agree that addressing these issues is in the long term public interest of all of us, that many of them represent areas of underinvestment, and that the application of the actuarial skill set could be of benefit?

The point is that the big problems do not just belong to Government, they belong to all of us, and some of them might prove a bit less intractable if more of us understood that and acted accordingly. All of the above interest areas have some impact on our collective future prosperity in the widest sense, which is more than can be said for some of the activities that presently keep us all busy.

In the wake of the present crisis, and compounding public ire, the root causes of widespread public anger and frustration remain to be addressed. Unfortunately for those in our own industry who hope that the public might quickly forget and move on, the aftermath of this crisis is going to have a long shelf life. MPs expenses provided a useful distraction for a while (and how we all vented our spleen about that), but Michael Martin still has his Lordship and the subject has been wrung dry. By contrast, the consequences of the hole that has been blown in the nation's confidence and its finances will reverberate for years, and when people begin to feel it in their pockets, in the form of higher taxes and lower public spending, we should expect them to rediscover a more fitting target for their resentment than MPs expenses.

They will not then need reminding how our industry binged itself, on a diet of unrestrained growth in debt, optimism, fickle foreign investment and ever-increasing product complexity, into a state of corpulence that considerably outweighs its net contribution to the good of society.

Such halcyon days, if that is what they were, are nearing their end. The UK is running out of fresh markets to exploit, and people are coming to realise that they have more pressing priorities than to indulge the excesses of a distended financial sector.

The financial crisis and a growing sense of awareness at the damage being wrought by free market ideology are ultimately going to leave our industry on the receiving end of a slimfast diet of reducing investment and changing public priorities. The result will be a long-overdue return to core values, a retrenchment of the industry towards servicing traditional finance needs and a move away from an emphasis on short term trading and speculation towards longer term planning and investment.

In a process that has already started, in the years to come public interest issues will increasingly prevail over corporate interests as a new social contract begins to emerge, one that reflects a far better balance of long term interests than our present doctrine affords.

This is a process from which the Profession is likely to emerge, in the absence of a fundamental change in its strategy, with less financial reward, fewer employment opportunities and less influence.

As the Profession returns from merger orbit to re-engage with real-world issues, it is my hope that the gravity of our present situation will not be lost on it. Recent events have scoured deeply into a veneer that was already wearing thin and offered proof, if it were still needed, that the twin objectives of serving a greater good and chasing ever greater wealth are fundamentally misaligned. The days of the Profession or any of its members being able to unequivocally defend both are numbered, which poses searching questions for the Profession as a whole and for each of us as its individual members.

It may be tempting, and it is certainly convenient, for us as individuals to believe that if we are fulfilling our mandatory CPD requirements, meeting our job objectives and helping our employers to meet their financial targets then we are fulfilling our Professional obligations.

In this paper I have sought to set out in detail the reasons why I believe this to be dangerously complacent thinking. Today's pressing public interest priorities extend far beyond those that any employer would be prepared to pay us a bonus for representing, and the Profession's present introspective focus on supporting its members' interests is not helping to redress collectively our underinvestment in matters of public interest as individuals.

What is to be the Profession's response? Is it going to realign itself to be at the forefront of developments in support of the move to more balanced priorities and a more sustainable future, or will we instead follow the example set by the people of Easter Island many years ago, building statues to fallen idols until the last tree is gone?

The disparity between the respective interests that the Profession seeks to serve continues to grow, yet the Profession continues to support failing paradigms and continues to have little of any significance to say about the failures of the industry in which it operates.

Radical thinking, long term vision and finding an independent voice of genuine moral authority are the ingredients needed for the Profession to break free from the historical baggage and introspective outlook that presently constrain it. Past precedents are not encouraging - this would represent a major departure from the Profession's traditional approach - but how much more incentive than that presented by current circumstance does the Profession need to make the leap?

Who is to make wise those who are required to have wisdom?

If our Profession's answer to this question continues to be 'someone else', a big opportunity will have been missed. At a time when people believe there to be a moral vacuum at the heart of Government and a moral vacuum at the heart of the Financial Services industry, for all its public interest rhetoric the Profession is failing to take a moral lead, despite the fact that it has a clear mandate to do so, and despite the fact that it could stand to benefit considerably from doing so.

There is no shortage of things to talk about, and there is no shortage of decisions to be taken. But there is a shortage of time. The World cannot afford to wait for us, and neither will it. If the Profession does not soon think outside a bigger box, it may yet find itself constrained forever inside a much smaller one.

In Conclusion

I have less invested in a sustainable future than many other people do, yet I have still chosen to write this paper. What conclusions could be drawn from this?

Well, perversely, it may just be that having less invested in a sustainable future was actually a help. I will never know, because I can of course only write from one perspective, but I suspect if my investment in future generations were greater I too might be looking for reasons to view the follies of the present in softer light. Nobody likes to think that they might be in any way culpable for compromising the quality of life of their own descendants, after all.

Yet I could have used the very fact that my investment *is* lower to justify choosing the soft option and staying silent. So have I lost the plot, or is there some other reason for me to be acting contrary to Galbraith's old notion ("...for the hope of an easy life causes those who know things are going quite wrong to say that things are fundamentally sound")?

I've been reflecting on that. The answer, I think, lies partly in conscience, partly in ire, and partly in my genuine belief that the Profession really could make a meaningful contribution, if only it could get its act together. But mostly it lies in a strong sense of history.

Having made it this far through my paper you could be forgiven for thinking that a sense of history had passed me by, but do not be fooled. I just happen to use little of it on my Profession. Most of it I spend in more profound reflection. Pondering, for example, that in nearly six hundred million years of earthly history there appear to have been only five other occasions when our planet's biodiversity has been put under greater threat than it is today. As far as we can tell none of the other events were self-inflicted, and certainly not by a species smart enough to have known better.

That dismays me more than any meagre investment I might make in my short time here could compensate for. But while it may already be too late to prevent the incidence of the sixth big event, it is still not too late to limit its severity. Everything is interlinked; small events can beget big consequences; this paper is the biggest investment in the cause of finding a better way, in any Professional capacity at least, that I felt able to make.

In these pages I have sought to examine the key threats that we face, and to consider the likely consequences of not addressing them. I have also tried to highlight the contradictions I see in the Profession's present vision and strategy and the means by which it has chosen to implement them.

In a wider context I have sought to expose the flaws in our current socio-economic model and the underlying drivers of increasing instability in our financial markets. I conclude that Government, too compromised by its own history, not radical enough in its thinking, not bold enough in its action and not honest enough in its discourse, is failing to address them.

I conclude that the general feeling of disillusionment and insecurity that currently pervades society isn't going to go away, for the simple reasons that a) it is entirely justified and b) little is being done to address its root causes.

I suggest that Government failure to address those concerns increases the importance of the role that other bodies with public interest obligations play, and I conclude that the Profession is presently failing in that role. One of the Profession's stated public interest passions is 'contributing to the debate on Government policy in financial matters'. Where has that contribution to debate been, in a year when it has been so desperately needed?

In these pages I have offered a number of suggestions as to how the Profession might set about building a more positive profile for itself, deploy its intellectual capital more effectively and better serve the public interest. While some of those suggestions represent more of a stretch than others, the pursuit of any of them would require a change in mindset from the one that the Profession presently exhibits.

The challenges we face are many and varied, complex and inter-related. I don't hold all the answers, but I do recognize that our continuing obsession with economic growth is part of the problem, not part of the solution, and in the circumstances I consider my Profession's apparent lack of willingness to engage in discussion on this and other important subjects touched upon in this paper to be an inexcusable abdication of responsibility.

While it is not too late for the Profession to reform itself into a more progressive force for good, in truth I am less optimistic about its capacity to do so now than I have ever been. The Profession's preoccupation with merger, insular attitude, introspective strategic focus and lack of worthwhile discourse in this time of crisis have all done little to inspire. More disillusioning, however, was the content of a recent Institute mailshot I received. A few weeks ago the latest set of Council Election papers landed on my doormat. I won't dwell on how reasonable it is to describe a process that offers up six candidates for five appointments as an election, but I will dwell on the nature of the choice, as evidenced by the content of the respective candidates' one page 'manifestos'.

All candidates made reference to members' interests. Five of them made reference to the merger, and business achievements were of course given prominence in the profiles. But what of the present financial crisis and its implications for the Profession? What of the public interest, at a time when it has never been under greater threat?

The momentary optimism I experienced upon reading of one nominee's desire to 'determine the real and underlying causes of what happened' and explore the 'viability of potential changes' proved just that: he was of course talking about the merger process, not the collapse of the World economy. Silly me.

In fact, there was not one single mention of either the financial crisis or the public interest in the entire pack. Crisis? What crisis?

When one listens to our Profession's leadership talk about how the world needs actuaries, and then one looks at how as a Profession we are presently investing most of our time, one can but marvel at the gulf. It would be laughable were it not so serious.

When I first began writing this paper, in the immediate aftermath of the near-collapse of our financial system, I had some optimism that at least from the wreckage some much-needed lessons would be learned, both inside and outside the Profession.

Nine months on, that optimism looks increasingly misplaced. Life on planet actuary seems to be continuing pretty much as normal, and life in our financial solar system is also striving to return to what was hitherto regarded as normal. In the wake of the crisis, such debate as is still taking place within the Profession seems to be far more about risk management than it is about the need for reform, and seems to have been parked with the Global Financial Crisis Group.

Meanwhile, back in the real world, while political expediency and desperation for revenue do at last appear to be stirring the Government to act (for example in relation to the taxation of bank bonuses and its belated backing of Lord Turner's call for the introduction of a levy on financial transactions), in no sense is it yet showing any appetite to address anything other than symptoms.

My posthumous congratulations yet again to Galbraith, then, for his insight into human nature appears to have passed another tough test.

Who is to make wise those who we require to have wisdom?

It is my hope this paper will be seen by at least some of those who read it as something of a wake-up call. I don't credit myself with enough influence to expect any tangible change in approach on the part of the Profession as a whole to result, though I do of course hope that the Profession will soon heed the many warning signs and change its ways.

If it doesn't, however, I do have a rather selfish insurance policy. That policy will vest when, from the confines of a more austere existence, and as the blanket judgement of future generations is passed about the particular follies and profligacies of this one, it will be on record, for those prepared to look, that the Profession of which I was a member did not share my vision, and the industry I served did not share my values.

For those of you who are not discomfited by the issues about which I write, I hope your complacency proves to be well-founded.

For those of you who are, I hope you can find an appropriate way of exercising your conscience. But don't take a leaf out of your Profession's book: silence ought not to be an option.

Once upon a time, when people asked what I did for a living I used to take some pride in telling them and hope that my answer might meet with some recognition. These days, I find myself hoping for a blank look and a quick change in the topic of conversation. And funnily enough, twenty five years on, that is still largely what I get.

How this paper is received inside the Profession will be my own gauge of whether that is ever likely to change.

How this paper is received by those outside the Profession who read it will be my gauge of just how detached the Profession has become from the reality of others.

In my less optimistic moments I am inclined to think that I already know the answers. I can only hope that I may yet be proved wrong.

On the Role of the Actuary in a Changing World

PRECIS

Set out below, in bullet point format and under appropriate headings, is a summary of the key points and recommendations made in this paper.

In reading this summary, please be mindful that my main aim in writing this paper is to promote debate, not to uniquely define problems or solutions. The paper's subject matter opens many avenues for discussion, and no one individual could hope to come up with the best possible course of action in respect of each.

While I have of course taken the opportunity to express my views, I consider it to be of more importance for the Profession as a whole to confront and debate the issues raised, agree a collective position, and agree an appropriate response.

Socio-Economic Context

- Our society is heading for a fall, and may be approaching a critical tipping point.
- Continuing to pursue an agenda driven by economic growth is detrimental to the long term public interest. A new balance of priorities is needed.
- Not only is our present economic model unable to deliver this, but it is in direct conflict with many of the priorities that now need to be addressed.
- Government is weak, its thinking is trapped by the needs of a short-term electoral cycle, mainstream parties have lost their moral authority, the expectations of the electorate are being mismanaged and no political party is articulating a cohesive vision for a sustainable future.
- The degree of global cooperation presently falls far short of that demanded by our collective situation. When the chips are down, too often Governments tend to act in their own short-term interests, and to the detriment of the long term greater good.
- In the absence of a change in socio-economic priorities and greater global co-operation, a combination of competition for increasingly scarce resource, polarisation in the distribution of wealth and the burden of unfulfilled expectation will lead to social disintegration and conflict.

Recommendations

1. **The Profession should reflect on how it can better use its influence to help support the urgent need for a move to a socio-economic model that is less driven by growth and profit and more focused on stability and sustainability.**
2. **The past is no longer a guide to the future, and the sophistication of our financial models has long since ceased to be the limiting factor in equipping actuaries to expedite their responsibilities. The Profession needs to start relying more on the application of long term vision, hard logic and common**

sense, and less on complex financial models that are based on failing paradigms and populated with unreliable assumptions.

3. The Profession should set up a semi-permanent policy group, with a more proactive and progressive mandate than that afforded the Global Financial Crisis Group, to develop the Profession's position in a number of pressing policy areas and on a number of pressing public interest issues.

4. To facilitate this the Profession needs to develop a more clearly defined and focused policy framework, be more active in its engagement in public discourse on relevant public interest issues of the day, and develop stronger links with the media to ensure its views gain exposure.

5. Global problems need global solutions, and the Profession should be more active in promoting stronger international links to help develop them.

6. In similar spirit the UK Profession could also better use its influence to deter the UK Government or Financial Services industry from adopting short term protectionist measures that are to the detriment of the wider long term public interest.

Industry-Specific

- As a result of the banking crisis, Financial Services is presently industry non-grata. This will not change until the industry is seen to put its own house in order.

- In the wake of that crisis, the gap in perceptions between those who lead the industry and the wider public who rely on its services has grown into a gulf of potentially irreparable proportions.

- A perceived lack of contrition and the absence of any substantive reform are exacerbating this trend.

- Continuing indefensible pay scales at the top end of the industry are also exacerbating this trend.

- Public trust in the Industry and in Government's ability to adequately supervise it has been shattered.

- Many industry interests are seeking to cast recent problems purely in banking terms, and as a one-off event. This is disingenuous. Industry problems run much deeper and reach far wider.

- Industry developments and investment trends have resulted in increased volatility in financial markets and increasingly frequent and dramatic departures from economic fundamentals.

- The banking crisis may be a one-off symptom, but its root causes are pervasive. Greater financial crises lie ahead and without reform the industry will not be well-equipped to weather the ensuing financial storm.

- Industry calls for the UK to remain 'competitive' in its tax, regulation and remuneration practices are misplaced. Tax, regulation and remuneration practices need reforming to be _fair_. The UK industry played a leading role in precipitating the crisis, and has thus far sought more to obstruct than embrace proposals aimed at addressing its root causes.

- This is a symptom of wider malaise, and evidence that many of the industry's present leaders are not fit to lead it into the more austere and socially-responsible future that awaits it.
- Industry scaremongering that restraint (on packages or activities) will lead to a mass exodus of irreplaceable talent is just that. There are plenty of talented people whose concept of nationhood isn't trumped by their greed, and a clearout of the industry's financially fickle and feckless would be no bad thing.
- The UK Profession's 20,000+ membership represents a considerable pool of intellectual capital. At a time when there are many pressing priorities in which it could be being invested, some of that capital is presently yielding a poor return.

Recommendations

7. **The Profession should better support initiatives to reform Financial Markets in order to reduce their volatility and ensure that they better serve the interests of society. In particular the Profession should either lend its weight to the FSA's proposals for a global Tobin tax on certain financial transactions and EU proposals to better regulate the activities of hedge funds, or come up with its own proposals.**

8. **The Profession should issue advisory guidance renouncing profit-related pay for all actuaries who work for financial institutions in a traditional actuarial capacity, thereby removing an obvious conflict of interest, underlining the Profession's independence and helping to restore its credibility.**

9. **In the circumstances the Profession as a whole and each of us as its individual members, ought to be reflecting on priorities and asking how our intellectual capital could be deployed to better effect. As Professor Garciano of the LSE so aptly noted, people tend to do what they are paid to do regardless of its worth to society. Plenty of actuaries should empathise with that, even though they may not care to admit it.**

10. **As individuals we need to speak out more against things we know to be either wrong or not in the long term public interest, from saving the planet to saving our industry from its own excesses to saving our collective reputation. Many of us seem to regard what is not in our individual job descriptions as someone else's problem or for the Profession as a whole to comment upon. It isn't, and it doesn't.**

11. **The Profession should recognise its risk management limitations, reflect on the extent to which modern-day financial markets and our present socio-economic model are exacerbating the risk management challenge, and seek to better manage the expectations of those who place reliance upon its risk assessments.**

12. **In support of its wider public interest obligations, the profession should contribute more to the analysis and management of risks that transcend corporate boundaries.**

- *In general*, the Profession is not demonstrating sufficient independence from the interests of those who employ its services.
- *In general*, the Profession is investing too much in promoting its own members interests and too little in promoting the long term public interest.
- In consequence, where there are conflicts of interest it is often the long term public interest that suffers. This is damaging to the Profession's reputation and runs contrary to its mandate.
- The Profession's public interest obligations are poorly defined, and beyond the specific job responsibilities of its individual members they are being poorly represented.
- A merger between Institute and Faculty would be an important first step for the Profession to begin to address these and other issues, but on its own a merger will change little.
- The merger process and the aftermath of the financial crisis have shown that the Profession's present strategy and policies are unfit to meet the challenges of a fast-changing World.
- The merger process has also shown that the Profession's decision-making criteria are also unfit to meet the challenges of a fast-changing World.
- The Profession should recognise that past paradigms are failing. The past is no longer a guide to the future, and there is increasing uncertainty in many of the assumptions that we traditionally use.
- The Profession sees wider risk management as a growth area, but in truth as actuaries we have traditionally been rather more effective at *analysing* risks than we have been at *managing* them.
- The Profession will only be in a position to build its credibility in the risk management arena when it has something constructive to say about the bigger risks we now face and how they could be better managed - and this will require a change in mindset.
- The Profession's policy framework is not sufficiently clearly defined, leaving people unclear not only about what it does but about what it stands for.
- The Profession's media presence is inadequate. An absence of initiatives leaving the news agenda left largely at the mercy of events, which in recent years have largely been driven by industry scandals.
- Traditional work areas are going to come under increasing pressure in years to come. Both the volume of work and its perceived value to society will reduce. This presents something of a problem.
- A significant proportion of work presently undertaken by actuaries amounts to a poor return on invested intellectual capital, at a time when there are many more worthwhile outlets for it. This presents something of an opportunity.
- Any significant change in the Profession's direction or expansion of its interest areas will need to be Profession-led. It is not going to happen by osmosis, or through an introspective strategy whose focus is on supporting members interests. The Profession's strategy is focused too much on serving the needs of its individual members, and too little on collective representation.

13. **If the Profession's 'merger paralysis' is to continue, perhaps the progressive majorities both north and south of the artificial divide should consider collective resignation and subscription to a new Professional body with a more progressive mandate and a constitution that better reflects the demands of the times.**

14. **The Profession's current strategy is too introspective. This is to the detriment of both the Profession's own long term interests and to the wider public interest. A change in direction is needed, with proportionately less focus on supporting individual members' needs and more focus on matters of collective policy and issues of wider public interest.**

15. **The Profession should reflect on how effective it has been in servicing its public interest obligations in recent years and consider what changes could be made to improve its effectiveness. The list of provocations in the Appendix to this paper was included to help promote much-needed debate on this subject.**

16. **As part of this process the Profession should better clarify the boundaries of its public interest responsibilities. That they are so loosely defined is in part why wider public interest issues are so poorly represented.**

17. **A more proactive strategy of media engagement is required to gain more public exposure and better promote the Profession's interests and long term objectives.**

18. **The Profession should consider introducing a mandatory public interest requirement for all qualified actuaries to address some of the limitations of the present CPD system and to provide a much-needed boost in its contribution to matters of wider public interest.**

Notes & References

1. "UK international Financial Services – The Future", May 2009
2. "The World Needs Actuaries", Ronnie Bowie, presentation to the Faculty of Actuaries, 6th October 2008
3. "The Road to Ruin", Francis Pereira, (The Actuary, May 2009)
4. "The Great Crash 1929", J.K.Galbraith (1954)
5. *The Guardian* Executive Pay Survey 2008
6. World Institute for Development & Economics, global study of wealth distribution 2006
7. "The Folly of Growth", New Scientist 18th October 2008
8. "Who Runs Britain", Robert Peston (Hodder, 2008)
9. Nathanael Fast & Serena Chen, US Journal of Psycholigical Science (Nov 2009)
10. Taxpayers Alliance Research Note 14, 13th July 2007
11. "The Theory of the Moral Sentiments", Adam Smith, (1759)
12. "Actuaries and the Media: How to Educate Journalists", Eric Short, paper presented to SIAS 5th November 1991

APPENDIX

The Public Interest in Practice - A Self-Assessment Guide

1. For each of the public interest scenarios below, consider whether:

(i) you agree with the premise (Yes/No/Don't know)
(ii) in your opinion it is a subject about which the Profession should engage in public discourse (Yes/No/Don't know)
(iii) if so, whether that view would best be expressed by individual members or by the Profession as a whole (Yes/No/Don't know)
(iv) how effective you believe the Profession has been to date in meeting its public interest obligations on this issue (1=not at all effective, 5=very effective)

(1) If our Profession takes a long term view, is it in the public interest for so many of its members to subscribe without question to incentive schemes based solely on short term profit?

(2) Convention has it that nobody saw the present crisis coming, but like most soundbites that is not strictly true. Gordon Brown may have convinced himself that cycles of boom and bust had come to an end, but should our Profession not have noted the warning signs (ballooning house prices, the escalation of debt, the increase in dubiously-rated SIVs etc)?

(3) As a Profession we have witnessed, indeed contributed to, an explosion in the range and complexity of financial products and services over the last twenty years. Has not much of this been of more benefit to the organisations that employ us than it has been to their customers?

(4) Given the wide range of different investment vehicles now available to investors in the financial services sector, and given the inherent unpredictability of financial markets, are the current levels of commission paid to some intermediaries for selling investment products defensible?

(5) In the game of relative investment performance there are winners and losers, but the game itself is zero sum around the base level of real long term growth. The decade leading up to the 2008 crash saw an explosion in private equity firms and hedge funds. A number of these made stellar returns stretching to billions of pounds. Is it not the case that in large part their gain has been the institutional investors' – and more particularly their customers – loss? As financial experts employed by those companies should we not have been doing more to promote better governance of that investment?

(6) Insurance is sold not bought, so the adage goes – but how much of that is because people no longer understand what they're buying? Is developing complex products then having to pay an army of financial advisers to sell them really in the public interest, and should the Profession not be doing more to promote greater transparency and simpler products?

(7) Over the last twenty years or so we have witnessed a gradual transfer of risk from companies that provide insurance to their customers who purchase it. That process has happened on a range of fronts. In the pensions industry for example by a move to money purchase arrangements, in the life industry by a move to reviewable protection policies and unitised investment products, and in general insurance by a significant increase in rating factors and growth in the use of NCD (for example in rating PMI policies). In most instances, was it not the case that instead of a balanced exposition of the pros and cons only the benefits were sold, resulting in widespread subsequent disaffection among those who lost out as a result of the changes?

(8) It is common practice for financial institutions to offer better terms to new customers than they offer to existing customers, even when there is no difference in the respective risk profiles of those customers. Is this not just unfair but inefficient, and ultimately to the detriment of the public as a whole?

(9) The present financial crisis is a symptom of systemic failure on a global scale. This failure has profound impact on the public interest and on our ability to effectively carry out our role. The Profession has set up a working party to look into the implications of the crisis, but the main objective of the group is to 'provide information'. Is this not too weak a response?

(10) The present financial crisis also provides evidence of the extent to which the gap between short term commercial interests and the wider public interest has grown in recent years. As a Profession we presume our morality equips us to strike an appropriate balance between the two, but a) are there not now enough individual examples of failure in our own recent history to suggest otherwise, and b) isn't it increasingly apparent that the degree of dysfunction in our present economic and financial systems is rendering those interests irreconcilable?

(11) The European Commission's proposals to cap hedge fund debt leverage and Adair Turner's proposals for a Tobin tax on certain types of financial transaction met with a cool response in the UK in general, and no response from the Actuarial Profession in particular. Yet is it not true that the level of hedge fund borrowing, the scale of hedge fund leverage and the sheer volume of short term trading activity are direct contributors to the scale of market volatility we now witness and to the scale of impact of the current financial crisis?

More widely:

2. **Do you believe that the Profession has been clear in setting out the nature of its public interest obligations and how it will meet them**

   Not at all clear   1   2   3   4   5   Very Clear

3. **In general, how effective do you think the Profession has been in fulfilling its public interest obligations in recent years**

   Not at all effective   1   2   3   4   5   Very Effective

4. **How supportive do you believe the Profession's current strategy is in enabling it to fulfil those obligations**

   Not at all effective   1   2   3   4   5   Very Effective

CPSIA information can be obtained at www.ICGtesting.com
Printed in the USA
LVOW032240170812

294717LV00001B/31/P